As a Man Thinketh

&

The Way of Peace

By James Allen

Wilder Publications, LLC.
PO Box 3005
Radford VA 24143-3005

ISBN 13: 978-1-51-54-38557

First Edition

James Allen

10 9 8 7 6 5 4 3 2 1

As a Man Thinketh

Mind is the Master power that moulds and makes,
And Man is Mind, and evermore he takes
The tool of Thought, and, shaping what he wills,
Brings forth a thousand joys, a thousand ills:—
He thinks in secret, and it comes to pass:
Environment is but his looking-glass.

FOREWORD

THIS little volume (the result of meditation and experience) is not intended as an exhaustive treatise on the much-written-upon subject of the power of thought. It is suggestive rather than explanatory, its object being to stimulate men and women to the discovery and perception of the truth that—

"They themselves are makers of themselves."

by virtue of the thoughts, which they choose and encourage; that mind is the master-weaver, both of the inner garment of character and the outer garment of circumstance, and that, as they may have hitherto woven in ignorance and pain they may now weave in enlightenment and happiness.

James Allen.
Broad Park Avenue,
Ilfracombe,
England

THOUGHT AND CHARACTER

THE aphorism, "As a man thinketh in his heart so is he," not only embraces the whole of a man's being, but is so comprehensive as to reach out to every condition and circumstance of his life. A man is literally *what he thinks*, his character being the complete sum of all his thoughts.

As the plant springs from, and could not be without, the seed, so every act of a man springs from the hidden seeds of thought, and could not have appeared without them. This applies equally to those acts called "spontaneous" and "unpremeditated" as to those, which are deliberately executed.

Act is the blossom of thought, and joy and suffering are its fruits; thus does a man garner in the sweet and bitter fruitage of his own husbandry.

"Thought in the mind hath made us, What we are By thought was wrought and built. If a man's mind Hath evil thoughts, pain comes on him as comes The wheel the ox behind....

..If one endure In purity of thought, joy follows him As his own shadow—sure."

Man is a growth by law, and not a creation by artifice, and cause and effect is as absolute and undeviating in the hidden realm of thought as in the world of visible and material things. A noble and Godlike character is not a thing of favour or chance, but is the natural result of continued effort in right thinking, the effect of long-cherished association with Godlike thoughts. An ignoble and bestial character, by the same process, is the result of the continued harbouring of grovelling thoughts.

Man is made or unmade by himself; in the armoury of thought he forges the weapons by which he destroys himself; he also fashions the tools with which he builds for himself heavenly mansions of joy and strength and peace. By the right choice and true application of thought, man ascends to the Divine Perfection; by the abuse and wrong application of thought, he descends below the level of the beast. Between these two extremes are all the grades of character, and man is their maker and master.

Of all the beautiful truths pertaining to the soul which have been restored and brought to light in this age, none is more gladdening or fruitful of divine promise and confidence than this—that man is the master of thought, the moulder of character, and the maker and shaper of condition, environment, and destiny.

As a being of Power, Intelligence, and Love, and the lord of his own thoughts, man holds the key to every situation, and contains within himself that transforming and regenerative agency by which he may make himself what he wills.

Man is always the master, even in his weaker and most abandoned state; but in his weakness and degradation he is the foolish master who misgoverns his "household." When he begins to reflect upon his condition, and to search diligently for the Law upon which his being is established, he then becomes the wise master, directing his energies with intelligence, and fashioning his thoughts to fruitful issues. Such is the *conscious* master, and man can only thus become by discovering *within himself* the laws of thought; which discovery is totally a matter of application, self analysis, and experience.

Only by much searching and mining, are gold and diamonds obtained, and man can find every truth connected with his being, if he will dig deep into the mine of his soul; and that he is the maker of his character, the moulder of his life, and the builder of his destiny, he may unerringly prove, if he will watch, control, and alter his thoughts, tracing their effects upon himself, upon others, and upon his life and circumstances, linking cause and effect by patient practice and investigation, and utilizing his every experience, even to the most trivial, everyday occurrence, as a means of obtaining that knowledge of himself which is Understanding, Wisdom, Power. In this direction, as in no other, is the law absolute that "He that seeketh findeth; and to him that knocketh it shall be opened;" for only by patience, practice, and ceaseless importunity can a man enter the Door of the Temple of Knowledge.

EFFECT OF THOUGHT ON CIRCUMSTANCES

MAN'S mind may be likened to a garden, which may be intelligently cultivated or allowed to run wild; but whether cultivated or neglected, it must, and will, *bring forth*. If no useful seeds are *put* into it, then an abundance of useless weed-seeds will *fall* therein, and will continue to produce their kind.

Just as a gardener cultivates his plot, keeping it free from weeds, and growing the flowers and fruits which he requires, so may a man tend the garden of his mind, weeding out all the wrong, useless, and impure thoughts, and cultivating toward perfection the flowers and fruits of right, useful, and pure thoughts. By pursuing this process, a man sooner or later discovers that he is the master-gardener of his soul, the director of his life. He also reveals, within himself, the laws of thought, and understands, with ever-increasing accuracy, how the thought-forces and mind elements operate in the shaping of his character, circumstances, and destiny.

Thought and character are one, and as character can only manifest and discover itself through environment and circumstance, the outer conditions of a person's life will always be found to be harmoniously related to his inner state. This does not mean that a man's circumstances at any given time are an indication of his *entire* character, but that those circumstances are so intimately connected with some vital thought-element within himself that, for the time being, they are indispensable to his development.

Every man is where he is by the law of his being; the thoughts which he has built into his character have brought him there, and in the arrangement of his life there is no element of chance, but all is the result of a law which cannot err. This is just as true of those who feel "out of harmony" with their surroundings as of those who are contented with them.

As a progressive and evolving being, man is where he is that he may learn that he may grow; and as he learns the spiritual lesson which any circumstance contains for him, it passes away and gives place to other circumstances.

Man is buffeted by circumstances so long as he believes himself to be the creature of outside conditions, but when he realizes that he is a creative power, and that he may command the hidden soil and seeds of his being out of which circumstances grow, he then becomes the rightful master of himself.

That circumstances grow out of thought every man knows who has for any length of time practised self-control and self-purification, for he will have noticed that the alteration in his circumstances has been in exact ratio with his altered mental condition. So true is this that when a man earnestly applies himself to remedy the defects in his character, and makes swift and marked progress, he passes rapidly through a succession of vicissitudes.

The soul attracts that which it secretly harbours; that which it loves, and also that which it fears; it reaches the height of its cherished aspirations; it falls to the level of its unchastened desires,—and circumstances are the means by which the soul receives its own.

Every thought-seed sown or allowed to fall into the mind, and to take root there, produces its own, blossoming sooner or later into act, and bearing its own fruitage of opportunity and circumstance. Good thoughts bear good fruit, bad thoughts bad fruit.

The outer world of circumstance shapes itself to the inner world of thought, and both pleasant and unpleasant external conditions are factors, which make for the ultimate good of the individual. As the reaper of his own harvest, man learns both by suffering and bliss.

Following the inmost desires, aspirations, thoughts, by which he allows himself to be dominated, (pursuing the will-o'-the-wisps of impure imaginings or steadfastly walking the highway of strong and high endeavour), a man at last arrives at their fruition and fulfilment in the outer conditions of his life. The laws of growth and adjustment everywhere obtains.

A man does not come to the almshouse or the jail by the tyranny of fate or circumstance, but by the pathway of grovelling thoughts and base desires. Nor does a pure-minded man fall suddenly into crime by stress of any mere external force; the criminal thought had long been secretly fostered in the heart, and the hour of opportunity revealed its gathered power. Circumstance does not make the man; it reveals him to himself No such conditions can exist as descending into vice and its attendant sufferings apart from vicious inclinations, or ascending into virtue and its pure happiness without the continued cultivation of virtuous aspirations; and man, therefore, as the lord and master of thought, is the maker of himself the shaper and author of environment. Even at birth the soul comes to its own and through every step of its earthly pilgrimage it attracts those combinations of conditions which reveal itself, which are the reflections of its own purity and, impurity, its strength and weakness.

Men do not attract that which they *want*, but that which they *are*. Their whims, fancies, and ambitions are thwarted at every step, but their inmost thoughts and desires are fed with their own food, be it foul or clean. The "divinity that shapes our ends" is in ourselves; it is our very self. Only himself manacles man: thought and action are the gaolers of Fate—they imprison, being base; they are also the angels of Freedom—they liberate, being noble. Not what he wishes and prays for does a man get, but what he justly earns. His wishes and prayers are only gratified and answered when they harmonize with his thoughts and actions.

In the light of this truth, what, then, is the meaning of "fighting against circumstances?" It means that a man is continually revolting against an *effect* without, while all the time he is nourishing and preserving its *cause* in his heart. That cause may take the form of a conscious vice or an unconscious weakness; but whatever it is, it stubbornly retards the efforts of its possessor, and thus calls aloud for remedy.

Men are anxious to improve their circumstances, but are unwilling to improve themselves; they therefore remain bound. The man who does not shrink from self-crucifixion can never fail to accomplish the object upon which his heart is set. This is as true of earthly as of heavenly things. Even the man whose sole object is to acquire wealth must be prepared to make great personal sacrifices before he can accomplish his object; and how much more so he who would realize a strong and well-poised life?

Here is a man who is wretchedly poor. He is extremely anxious that his surroundings and home comforts should be improved, yet all the time he shirks his work, and considers he is justified in trying to deceive his employer on the ground of the insufficiency of his wages. Such a man does not understand the simplest rudiments of those principles which are the basis of true prosperity, and is not only totally unfitted to rise out of his wretchedness, but is actually attracting to himself a still deeper wretchedness by dwelling in, and acting out, indolent, deceptive, and unmanly thoughts.

Here is a rich man who is the victim of a painful and persistent disease as the result of gluttony. He is willing to give large sums of money to get rid of it, but he will not sacrifice his gluttonous desires. He wants to gratify his taste for rich and unnatural viands and have his health as well. Such a man is totally unfit to have health, because he has not yet learned the first principles of a healthy life.

Here is an employer of labour who adopts crooked measures to avoid paying the regulation wage, and, in the hope of making larger profits, reduces the wages of his workpeople. Such a man is altogether unfitted for prosperity, and when he finds himself bankrupt, both as regards reputation and riches, he blames circumstances, not knowing that he is the sole author of his condition.

I have introduced these three cases merely as illustrative of the truth that man is the causer (though nearly always is unconsciously) of his circumstances, and that, whilst aiming at a good end, he is continually frustrating its accomplishment by encouraging thoughts and desires which cannot possibly harmonize with that end. Such cases could be multiplied and varied almost indefinitely, but this is not necessary, as the reader can, if he so resolves, trace the action of the laws of thought in his own mind and life, and until this is done, mere external facts cannot serve as a ground of reasoning.

Circumstances, however, are so complicated, thought is so deeply rooted, and the conditions of happiness vary so, vastly with individuals, that a man's entire soul-condition (although it may be known to himself) cannot be judged by another from the external aspect of his life alone. A man may be honest in certain directions, yet suffer privations; a man may be dishonest in certain directions, yet acquire wealth; but the conclusion usually formed that the one man fails *because of his particular honesty*, and that the other *prospers because of his particular dishonesty*, is the result of a superficial judgment, which assumes that the dishonest man is almost totally corrupt, and the honest man almost entirely virtuous. In the light of a deeper knowledge and wider experience such judgment is found to be erroneous. The dishonest man may have some admirable virtues, which the other does, not possess; and the honest man obnoxious vices which are absent in the other. The honest man reaps the good results of his honest thoughts and acts; he also brings upon himself the sufferings, which his vices produce. The dishonest man likewise garners his own suffering and happiness.

It is pleasing to human vanity to believe that one suffers because of one's virtue; but not until a man has extirpated every sickly, bitter, and impure thought from his mind, and washed every sinful stain from his soul, can he be in a position to know and declare that his sufferings are the result of his good, and not of his bad qualities; and on the way to, yet long before he has reached, that supreme perfection, he will have found, working in his mind and life, the Great Law which is absolutely just, and which cannot, therefore, give good for evil, evil for good. Possessed of such knowledge, he will then know, looking back upon his past ignorance and blindness, that his life is, and always was, justly ordered, and that all his past experiences, good and bad, were the equitable outworking of his evolving, yet unevolved self.

Good thoughts and actions can never produce bad results; bad thoughts and actions can never produce good results. This is but saying that nothing can come from corn but corn, nothing from nettles but nettles. Men understand this law in the natural world, and work with it; but few understand it in the mental and moral world (though its operation there is just as simple and undeviating), and they, therefore, do not co-operate with it.

Suffering is *always* the effect of wrong thought in some direction. It is an indication that the individual is out of harmony with himself, with the Law of his being. The sole and supreme use of suffering is to purify, to burn out all that is useless and impure. Suffering ceases for him who is pure. There could be no object in burning gold after the dross had been removed, and a perfectly pure and enlightened being could not suffer.

The circumstances, which a man encounters with suffering, are the result of his own mental in harmony. The circumstances, which a man encounters with blessedness, are the result of his own mental harmony. Blessedness, not material possessions, is the measure of right thought; wretchedness, not lack of material possessions, is the measure of wrong thought. A man may be cursed and rich; he may be blessed and poor. Blessedness and riches are only joined together when the riches are rightly and wisely used; and the poor man only descends into wretchedness when he regards his lot as a burden unjustly imposed.

Indigence and indulgence are the two extremes of wretchedness. They are both equally unnatural and the result of mental disorder. A man is not rightly conditioned until he is a happy, healthy, and prosperous being; and happiness, health, and prosperity are the result of a harmonious adjustment of the inner with the outer, of the man with his surroundings.

A man only begins to be a man when he ceases to whine and revile, and commences to search for the hidden justice which regulates his life. And as he adapts his mind to that regulating factor, he ceases to accuse others as the cause of his condition, and builds himself up in strong and noble thoughts; ceases to kick against circumstances, but begins to *use* them as aids to his more rapid progress, and as a means of discovering the hidden powers and possibilities within himself.

Law, not confusion, is the dominating principle in the universe; justice, not injustice, is the soul and substance of life; and righteousness, not corruption, is the moulding and moving force in the spiritual government of the world. This being so, man has but to right himself to find that the universe is right; and during the process of putting himself right he will find that as he alters his thoughts towards things and other people, things and other people will alter towards him.

The proof of this truth is in every person, and it therefore admits of easy investigation by systematic introspection and self-analysis. Let a man radically alter his thoughts, and he will be astonished at the rapid transformation it will effect in the material conditions of his life. Men imagine that thought can be kept secret, but it cannot; it rapidly crystallizes into habit, and habit solidifies into circumstance. Bestial thoughts crystallize into habits of drunkenness and sensuality, which solidify into circumstances of destitution and disease: impure thoughts of every kind crystallize into enervating and confusing habits, which solidify into distracting and adverse circumstances: thoughts of fear, doubt, and indecision crystallize into weak, unmanly, and irresolute habits, which solidify into circumstances of failure, indigence, and slavish dependence: lazy thoughts crystallize into habits of uncleanliness and dishonesty, which solidify into circumstances of foulness and beggary: hateful and condemnatory thoughts crystallize into habits of accusation and violence, which solidify into circumstances of injury and persecution: selfish thoughts of all kinds crystallize into habits of self-seeking, which solidify into circumstances more or less distressing. On the other hand, beautiful thoughts of all kinds crystallize into habits of grace and kindliness, which solidify into genial and sunny circumstances: pure thoughts crystallize into habits of temperance and self-control, which solidify into circumstances of repose and peace: thoughts of courage, self-reliance, and decision crystallize into manly habits, which solidify into circumstances of success, plenty, and freedom: energetic thoughts crystallize into habits of cleanliness and industry, which solidify into circumstances of pleasantness: gentle and forgiving thoughts crystallize into habits of gentleness, which solidify into protective and preservative circumstances: loving and unselfish thoughts crystallize into habits of self-forgetfulness for others, which solidify into circumstances of sure and abiding prosperity and true riches.

A particular train of thought persisted in, be it good or bad, cannot fail to produce its results on the character and circumstances. A man cannot *directly* choose his circumstances, but he can choose his thoughts, and so indirectly, yet surely, shape his circumstances.

Nature helps every man to the gratification of the thoughts, which he most encourages, and opportunities are presented which will most speedily bring to the surface both the good and evil thoughts.

Let a man cease from his sinful thoughts, and all the world will soften towards him, and be ready to help him; let him put away his weakly and sickly thoughts, and lo, opportunities will spring up on every hand to aid his strong resolves; let him encourage good thoughts, and no hard fate shall bind him down to wretchedness and shame. The world is your kaleidoscope, and the varying combinations of colours, which at every succeeding moment it presents to you are the exquisitely adjusted pictures of your ever-moving thoughts.

"So You will be what you will to be;
Let failure find its false content
In that poor word, 'environment,'
But spirit scorns it, and is free.

"It masters time, it conquers space;
It cowes that boastful trickster, Chance,
And bids the tyrant Circumstance
Uncrown, and fill a servant's place.

"The human Will, that force unseen,
The offspring of a deathless Soul,
Can hew a way to any goal,
Though walls of granite intervene.

"Be not impatient in delays
But wait as one who understands;
When spirit rises and commands
The gods are ready to obey."

EFFECT OF THOUGHT ON HEALTH AND THE BODY

THE body is the servant of the mind. It obeys the operations of the mind, whether they be deliberately chosen or automatically expressed. At the bidding of unlawful thoughts the body sinks rapidly into disease and decay; at the command of glad and beautiful thoughts it becomes clothed with youthfulness and beauty.

Disease and health, like circumstances, are rooted in thought. Sickly thoughts will express themselves through a sickly body. Thoughts of fear have been known to kill a man as speedily as a bullet, and they are continually killing thousands of people just as surely though less rapidly. The people who live in fear of disease are the people who get it. Anxiety quickly demoralizes the whole body, and lays it open to the, entrance of disease; while impure thoughts, even if not physically indulged, will soon shatter the nervous system.

Strong, pure, and happy thoughts build up the body in vigour and grace. The body is a delicate and plastic instrument, which responds readily to the thoughts by which it is impressed, and habits of thought will produce their own effects, good or bad, upon it.

Men will continue to have impure and poisoned blood, so long as they propagate unclean thoughts. Out of a clean heart comes a clean life and a clean body. Out of a defiled mind proceeds a defiled life and a corrupt body. Thought is the fount of action, life, and manifestation; make the fountain pure, and all will be pure.

Change of diet will not help a man who will not change his thoughts. When a man makes his thoughts pure, he no longer desires impure food.

Clean thoughts make clean habits. The so-called saint who does not wash his body is not a saint. He who has strengthened and purified his thoughts does not need to consider the malevolent microbe.

If you would protect your body, guard your mind. If you would renew your body, beautify your mind. Thoughts of malice, envy, disappointment, despondency, rob the body of its health and grace. A sour face does not come by chance; it is made by sour thoughts. Wrinkles that mar are drawn by folly, passion, and pride.

I know a woman of ninety-six who has the bright, innocent face of a girl. I know a man well under middle age whose face is drawn into inharmonious contours. The one is the result of a sweet and sunny disposition; the other is the outcome of passion and discontent.

As you cannot have a sweet and wholesome abode unless you admit the air and sunshine freely into your rooms, so a strong body and a bright, happy, or serene countenance can only result from the free admittance into the mind of thoughts of joy and goodwill and serenity.

On the faces of the aged there are wrinkles made by sympathy, others by strong and pure thought, and others are carved by passion: who cannot distinguish them? With those who have lived righteously, age is calm, peaceful, and softly mellowed, like the setting sun. I have recently seen a philosopher on his deathbed. He was not old except in years. He died as sweetly and peacefully as he had lived.

There is no physician like cheerful thought for dissipating the ills of the body; there is no comforter to compare with goodwill for dispersing the shadows of grief and sorrow. To live continually in thoughts of ill will, cynicism, suspicion, and envy, is to be confined in a self made prison-hole. But to think well of all, to be cheerful with all, to patiently learn to find the good in all—such unselfish thoughts are the very portals of heaven; and to dwell day by day in thoughts of peace toward every creature will bring abounding peace to their possessor.

THOUGHT AND PURPOSE

UNTIL thought is linked with purpose there is no intelligent accomplishment. With the majority the bark of thought is allowed to "drift" upon the ocean of life. Aimlessness is a vice, and such drifting must not continue for him who would steer clear of catastrophe and destruction.

They who have no central purpose in their life fall an easy prey to petty worries, fears, troubles, and self-pityings, all of which are indications of weakness, which lead, just as surely as deliberately planned sins (though by a different route), to failure, unhappiness, and loss, for weakness cannot persist in a power evolving universe.

A man should conceive of a legitimate purpose in his heart, and set out to accomplish it. He should make this purpose the centralizing point of his thoughts. It may take the form of a spiritual ideal, or it may be a worldly object, according to his nature at the time being; but whichever it is, he should steadily focus his thought-forces upon the object, which he has set before him. He should make this purpose his supreme duty, and should devote himself to its attainment, not allowing his thoughts to wander away into ephemeral fancies, longings, and imaginings. This is the royal road to self-control and true concentration of thought. Even if he fails again and again to accomplish his purpose (as he necessarily must until weakness is overcome), the *strength of character gained* will be the measure of *his true* success, and this will form a new starting-point for future power and triumph.

Those who are not prepared for the apprehension of a *great* purpose should fix the thoughts upon the faultless performance of their duty, no matter how insignificant their task may appear. Only in this way can the thoughts be gathered and focussed, and resolution and energy be developed, which being done, there is nothing which may not be accomplished.

The weakest soul, knowing its own weakness, and believing this truth *that strength can only be developed by effort and practice*, will, thus believing, at once begin to exert itself, and, adding effort to effort, patience to patience, and strength to strength, will never cease to develop, and will at last grow divinely strong.

As the physically weak man can make himself strong by careful and patient training, so the man of weak thoughts can make them strong by exercising himself in right thinking.

To put away aimlessness and weakness, and to begin to think with purpose, is to enter the ranks of those strong ones who only recognize failure as one of the pathways to attainment; who make all conditions serve them, and who think strongly, attempt fearlessly, and accomplish masterfully.

Having conceived of his purpose, a man should mentally mark out a *straight* pathway to its achievement, looking neither to the right nor the left. Doubts and fears should be rigorously excluded; they are disintegrating elements, which break up the straight line of effort, rendering it crooked, ineffectual, useless. Thoughts of doubt and fear never accomplished anything, and never can. They always lead to failure. Purpose, energy, power to do, and all strong thoughts cease when doubt and fear creep in.

The will to do springs from the knowledge that we *can* do. Doubt and fear are the great enemies of knowledge, and he who encourages them, who does not slay them. thwarts himself at every step.

He who has conquered doubt and fear has conquered failure. His every, thought is allied with power, and all difficulties are bravely met and wisely overcome. His purposes are seasonably planted, and they bloom and bring forth fruit, which does not fall prematurely to the ground.

Thought allied fearlessly to purpose becomes creative force: he who *knows* this is ready to become something higher and stronger than a mere bundle of wavering thoughts and fluctuating sensations; he who *does* this has become the conscious and intelligent wielder of his mental powers.

THE THOUGHT-FACTOR IN ACHIEVEMENT

ALL that a man achieves and all that he fails to achieve is the direct result of his own thoughts. In a justly ordered universe, where loss of equipoise would mean total destruction, individual responsibility must be absolute. A man's weakness and strength, purity and impurity, are his own, and not another man's; they are brought about by himself, and not by another; and they can only be altered by himself, never by another. His condition is also his own, and not another man's. His suffering and his happiness are evolved from within. As he thinks, so he is; as he continues to think, so he remains.

A strong man cannot help a weaker unless that weaker is *willing* to be helped, and even then the weak man must become strong of himself; he must, by his own efforts, develop the strength which he admires in another. None but himself can alter his condition.

It has been usual for men to think and to say, "Many men are slaves because one is an oppressor; let us hate the oppressor." Now, however, there is amongst an increasing few a tendency to reverse this judgment, and to say, "One man is an oppressor because many are slaves; let us despise the slaves."

The truth is that oppressor and slave are co-operators in ignorance, and, while seeming to afflict each other, are in reality afflicting themselves. A perfect Knowledge perceives the action of law in the weakness of the oppressed and the misapplied power of the oppressor; a perfect Love, seeing the suffering, which both states entail, condemns neither; a perfect Compassion embraces both oppressor and oppressed.

He who has conquered weakness, and has put away all selfish thoughts, belongs neither to oppressor nor oppressed. He is free.

A man can only rise, conquer, and achieve by lifting up his thoughts. He can only remain weak, and abject, and miserable by refusing to lift up his thoughts.

Before a man can achieve anything, even in worldly things, he must lift his thoughts above slavish animal indulgence. He may not, in order to succeed, give up all animality and selfishness, by any means; but a portion of it must, at least, be sacrificed. A man whose first thought is bestial indulgence could neither think clearly nor plan methodically; he could not find and develop his latent resources, and would fail in any undertaking. Not having commenced to manfully control his thoughts, he is not in a position to control affairs and to adopt serious responsibilities. He is not fit to act independently and stand alone. But he is limited only by the thoughts, which he chooses.

There can be no progress, no achievement without sacrifice, and a man's worldly success will be in the measure that he sacrifices his confused animal thoughts, and fixes his mind on the development of his plans, and the strengthening of his resolution and self-reliance. And the higher he lifts his thoughts, the more manly, upright, and righteous he becomes, the greater will be his success, the more blessed and enduring will be his achievements.

The universe does not favour the greedy, the dishonest, the vicious, although on the mere surface it may sometimes appear to do so; it helps the honest, the magnanimous, the virtuous. All the great Teachers of the ages have declared this in varying forms, and to prove and know it a man has but to persist in making himself more and more virtuous by lifting up his thoughts.

Intellectual achievements are the result of thought consecrated to the search for knowledge, or for the beautiful and true in life and nature. Such achievements may be sometimes connected with vanity and ambition, but they are not the outcome of those characteristics; they are the natural outgrowth of long and arduous effort, and of pure and unselfish thoughts.

Spiritual achievements are the consummation of holy aspirations. He who lives constantly in the conception of noble and lofty thoughts, who dwells upon all that is pure and unselfish, will, as surely as the sun reaches its zenith and the moon its full, become wise and noble in character, and rise into a position of influence and blessedness.

Achievement, of whatever kind, is the crown of effort, the diadem of thought. By the aid of self-control, resolution, purity, righteousness, and well-directed thought a man ascends; by the aid of animality, indolence, impurity, corruption, and confusion of thought a man descends.

A man may rise to high success in the world, and even to lofty altitudes in the spiritual realm, and again descend into weakness and wretchedness by allowing arrogant, selfish, and corrupt thoughts to take possession of him.

Victories attained by right thought can only be maintained by watchfulness. Many give way when success is assured, and rapidly fall back into failure.

All achievements, whether in the business, intellectual, or spiritual world, are the result of definitely directed thought, are governed by the same law and are of the same method; the only difference lies in *the object of attainment*.

He who would accomplish little must sacrifice little; he who would achieve much must sacrifice much; he who would attain highly must sacrifice greatly.

VISIONS AND IDEALS

THE dreamers are the saviours of the world. As the visible world is sustained by the invisible, so men, through all their trials and sins and sordid vocations, are nourished by the beautiful visions of their solitary dreamers. Humanity cannot forget its dreamers; it cannot let their ideals fade and die; it lives in them; it knows them as they *realities* which it shall one day see and know.

Composer, sculptor, painter, poet, prophet, sage, these are the makers of the after-world, the architects of heaven. The world is beautiful because they have lived; without them, labouring humanity would perish.

He who cherishes a beautiful vision, a lofty ideal in his heart, will one day realize it. Columbus cherished a vision of another world, and he discovered it; Copernicus fostered the vision of a multiplicity of worlds and a wider universe, and he revealed it; Buddha beheld the vision of a spiritual world of stainless beauty and perfect peace, and he entered into it.

Cherish your visions; cherish your ideals; cherish the music that stirs in your heart, the beauty that forms in your mind, the loveliness that drapes your purest thoughts, for out of them will grow all delightful conditions, all, heavenly environment; of these, if you but remain true to them, your world will at last be built.

To desire is to obtain; to aspire is to, achieve. Shall man's basest desires receive the fullest measure of gratification, and his purest aspirations starve for lack of sustenance? Such is not the Law: such a condition of things can never obtain: "ask and receive."

Dream lofty dreams, and as you dream, so shall you become. Your Vision is the promise of what you shall one day be; your Ideal is the prophecy of what you shall at last unveil.

The greatest achievement was at first and for a time a dream. The oak sleeps in the acorn; the bird waits in the egg; and in the highest vision of the soul a waking angel stirs. Dreams are the seedlings of realities.

Your circumstances may be uncongenial, but they shall not long remain so if you but perceive an Ideal and strive to reach it. You cannot travel *within* and stand still *without*. Here is a youth hard pressed by poverty and labour; confined long hours in an unhealthy workshop; unschooled, and lacking all the arts of refinement. But he dreams of better things; he thinks of intelligence, of refinement, of grace and beauty. He conceives of, mentally builds up, an ideal condition of life; the vision of a wider liberty and a larger scope takes possession of him; unrest urges him to action, and he utilizes all his spare time and means, small though they are, to the development of his latent powers and resources. Very soon so altered has his mind become that the workshop can no longer hold him. It has become so out of harmony with his mentality that it falls out of his life as a garment is cast aside, and, with the growth of opportunities, which fit the scope of his expanding powers, he passes out of it forever. Years later we see this youth as a full-grown man. We find him a master of certain forces of the mind, which he wields with worldwide influence and almost unequalled power. In his hands he holds the cords of gigantic responsibilities; he speaks, and lo, lives are changed; men and women hang upon his words and remould their characters, and, sunlike, he becomes the fixed and luminous centre round which innumerable destinies revolve. He has realized the Vision of his youth. He has become one with his Ideal.

And you, too, youthful reader, will realize the Vision (not the idle wish) of your heart, be it base or beautiful, or a mixture of both, for you will always gravitate toward that which you, secretly, most love. Into your hands will be placed the exact results of your own thoughts; you will receive that which you earn; no more, no less. Whatever your present environment may be, you will fall, remain, or rise with your thoughts, your Vision, your Ideal. You will become as small as your controlling desire; as great as your dominant aspiration: in the beautiful words of Stanton Kirkham Davis, "You may be keeping accounts, and presently you shall walk out of the door that for so long has seemed to you the barrier of your ideals, and shall find yourself before an audience—the pen still behind your ear, the ink stains on your fingers and then and there shall pour out the torrent of your inspiration. You may be driving sheep, and you shall wander to the city-bucolic and open-mouthed; shall wander under the intrepid guidance of the spirit into the studio of the master, and after a time he shall say, 'I have nothing more to teach you.' And now you have become the master, who did so recently dream of great things while driving sheep. You shall lay down the saw and the plane to take upon yourself the regeneration of the world."

The thoughtless, the ignorant, and the indolent, seeing only the apparent effects of things and not the things themselves, talk of luck, of fortune, and chance. Seeing a man grow rich, they say, "How lucky he is!" Observing another become intellectual, they exclaim, "How highly favoured he is!" And noting the saintly character and wide influence of another, they remark, "How chance aids him at every turn!" They do not see the trials and failures and struggles which these men have voluntarily encountered in order to gain their experience; have no knowledge of the sacrifices they have made, of the undaunted efforts they have put forth, of the faith they have exercised, that they might overcome the apparently insurmountable, and realize the Vision of their heart. They do not know the darkness and the heartaches; they only see the light and joy, and call it "luck". They do not see the long and arduous journey, but only behold the pleasant goal, and call it "good fortune," do not understand the process, but only perceive the result, and call it chance.

In all human affairs there are *efforts*, and there are *results*, and the strength of the effort is the measure of the result. Chance is not. Gifts, powers, material, intellectual, and spiritual possessions are the fruits of effort; they are thoughts completed, objects accomplished, visions realized.

The Vision that you glorify in your mind, the Ideal that you enthrone in your heart—this you will build your life by, this you will become.

SERENITY

CALMNESS of mind is one of the beautiful jewels of wisdom. It is the result of long and patient effort in self-control. Its presence is an indication of ripened experience, and of a more than ordinary knowledge of the laws and operations of thought.

A man becomes calm in the measure that he understands himself as a thought evolved being, for such knowledge necessitates the understanding of others as the result of thought, and as he develops a right understanding, and sees more and more clearly the internal relations of things by the action of cause and effect he ceases to fuss and fume and worry and grieve, and remains poised, steadfast, serene.

The calm man, having learned how to govern himself, knows how to adapt himself to others; and they, in turn, reverence his spiritual strength, and feel that they can learn of him and rely upon him. The more tranquil a man becomes, the greater is his success, his influence, his power for good. Even the ordinary trader will find his business prosperity increase as he develops a greater self-control and equanimity, for people will always prefer to deal with a man whose demeanour is strongly equable.

The strong, calm man is always loved and revered. He is like a shade-giving tree in a thirsty land, or a sheltering rock in a storm. "Who does not love a tranquil heart, a sweet-tempered, balanced life? It does not matter whether it rains or shines, or what changes come to those possessing these blessings, for they are always sweet, serene, and calm. That exquisite poise of character, which we call serenity is the last lesson of culture, the fruitage of the soul. It is precious as wisdom, more to be desired than gold—yea, than even fine gold. How insignificant mere money seeking looks in comparison with a serene life—a life that dwells in the ocean of Truth, beneath the waves, beyond the reach of tempests, in the Eternal Calm!

"How many people we know who sour their lives, who ruin all that is sweet and beautiful by explosive tempers, who destroy their poise of character, and make bad blood! It is a question whether the great majority of people do not ruin their lives and mar their happiness by lack of self-control. How few people we meet in life who are well balanced, who have that exquisite poise which is characteristic of the finished character!

Yes, humanity surges with uncontrolled passion, is tumultuous with ungoverned grief, is blown about by anxiety and doubt only the wise man, only he whose thoughts are controlled and purified, makes the winds and the storms of the soul obey him.

Tempest-tossed souls, wherever ye may be, under whatsoever conditions ye may live, know this in the ocean of life the isles of Blessedness are smiling, and the sunny shore of your ideal awaits your coming. Keep your hand firmly upon the helm of thought. In the bark of your soul reclines the commanding Master; He does but sleep: wake Him. Self-control is strength; Right Thought is mastery; Calmness is power. Say unto your heart, "Peace, be still!"

The Way of Peace

THE POWER OF MEDITATION

Spiritual meditation is the pathway to Divinity. It is the mystic ladder which reaches from earth to heaven, from error to Truth, from pain to peace. Every saint has climbed it; every sinner must sooner or later come to it, and every weary pilgrim that turns his back upon self and the world, and sets his face resolutely toward the Father's Home, must plant his feet upon its golden rounds. Without its aid you cannot grow into the divine state, the divine likeness, the divine peace, and the fadeless glories and unpolluting joys of Truth will remain hidden from you.

Meditation is the intense dwelling, in thought, upon an idea or theme, with the object of thoroughly comprehending it, and whatsoever you constantly meditate upon you will not only come to understand, but will grow more and more into its likeness, for it will become incorporated into your very being, will become, in fact, your very self. If, therefore, you constantly dwell upon that which is selfish and debasing, you will ultimately become selfish and debased; if you ceaselessly think upon that which is pure and unselfish you will surely become pure and unselfish.

Tell me what that is upon which you most frequently and intensely think, that to which, in your silent hours, your soul most naturally turns, and I will tell you to what place of pain or peace you are traveling, and whether you are growing into the likeness of the divine or the bestial.

There is an unavoidable tendency to become literally the embodiment of that quality upon which one most constantly thinks. Let, therefore, the object of your meditation be above and not below, so that every time you revert to it in thought you will be lifted up; let it be pure and unmixed with any selfish element; so shall your heart become purified and drawn nearer to Truth, and not defiled and dragged more hopelessly into error.

Meditation, in the spiritual sense in which I am now using it, is the secret of all growth in spiritual life and knowledge. Every prophet, sage, and savior became such by the power of meditation. Buddha meditated upon the Truth until he could say, "I am the Truth." Jesus brooded upon the Divine immanence until at last he could declare, "I and my Father are One."

Meditation centered upon divine realities is the very essence and soul of prayer. It is the silent reaching of the soul toward the Eternal. Mere petitionary prayer without meditation is a body without a soul, and is powerless to lift the mind and heart above sin and affliction. If you are daily praying for wisdom, for peace, for loftier purity and a fuller realization of Truth, and that for which you pray is still far from you, it means that you are praying for one thing while living out in thought and act another. If you will cease from such waywardness, taking your mind off those things the selfish clinging to which debars you from the possession of the stainless realities for which you pray: if you will no longer ask God to grant you that which you do not deserve, or to bestow upon you that love and compassion which you refuse to bestow upon others, but will commence to think and act in the spirit of Truth, you will day by day be growing into those realities, so that ultimately you will become one with them.

He who would secure any worldly advantage must be willing to work vigorously for it, and he would be foolish indeed who, waiting with folded hands, expected it to come to him for the mere asking. Do not then vainly imagine that you can obtain the heavenly possessions without making an effort. Only when you commence to work earnestly in the Kingdom of Truth will you be allowed to partake of the Bread of Life, and when you have, by patient and uncomplaining effort, earned the spiritual wages for which you ask, they will not be withheld from you.

If you really seek Truth, and not merely your own gratification; if you love it above all worldly pleasures and gains; more, even, than happiness itself, you will be willing to make the effort necessary for its achievement.

If you would be freed from sin and sorrow; if you would taste of that spotless purity for which you sigh and pray; if you would realize wisdom and knowledge, and would enter into the possession of profound and abiding peace, come now and enter the path of meditation, and let the supreme object of your meditation be Truth.

At the outset, meditation must be distinguished from *idle reverie*. There is nothing dreamy and unpractical about it. It is *a process of searching and uncompromising thought which allows nothing to remain but the simple and naked truth*. Thus meditating you will no longer strive to build yourself up in your prejudices, but, forgetting self, you will remember only that you are seeking the Truth. And so you will remove, one by one, the errors which you have built around yourself in the past, and will patiently wait for the revelation of Truth which will come when your errors have been sufficiently removed. In the silent humility of your heart you will realize that

"There is an inmost centre in us all
Where Truth abides in fulness; and around,
Wall upon wall, the gross flesh hems it in;
This perfect, clear perception, which is Truth,
A baffling and perverting carnal mesh
Blinds it, and makes all error; and to know,
Rather consists in opening out a way
Whence the imprisoned splendour may escape,
Than in effecting entry for a light
Supposed to be without."

Select some portion of the day in which to meditate, and keep that period sacred to your purpose. The best time is the very early morning when the spirit of repose is upon everything. All natural conditions will then be in your favor; the passions, after the long bodily fast of the night, will be subdued, the excitements and worries of the previous day will have died away, and the mind, strong and yet restful, will be receptive to spiritual instruction. Indeed, one of the first efforts you will be called upon to make will be to shake off lethargy and indulgence, and if you refuse you will be unable to advance, for the demands of the spirit are imperative.

To be spiritually awakened is also to be mentally and physically awakened. The sluggard and the self-indulgent can have no knowledge of Truth. He who, possessed of health and strength, wastes the calm, precious hours of the silent morning in drowsy indulgence is totally unfit to climb the heavenly heights.

He whose awakening consciousness has become alive to its lofty possibilities, who is beginning to shake off the darkness of ignorance in which the world is enveloped, rises before the stars have ceased their vigil, and, grappling with the darkness within his soul, strives, by holy aspiration, to perceive the light of Truth while the unawakened world dreams on.

"The heights by great men reached and kept,
Were not attained by sudden flight,
But they, while their companions slept,
Were toiling upward in the night."

No saint, no holy man, no teacher of Truth ever lived who did not rise early in the morning. Jesus habitually rose early, and climbed the solitary mountains to engage in holy communion. Buddha always rose an hour before sunrise and engaged in meditation, and all his disciples were enjoined to do the same.

If you have to commence your daily duties at a very early hour, and are thus debarred from giving the early morning to systematic meditation, try to give an hour at night, and should this, by the length and laboriousness of your daily task be denied you, you need not despair, for you may turn your thoughts upward in holy meditation in the intervals of your work, or in those few idle minutes which you now waste in aimlessness; and should your work be of that kind which becomes by practice automatic, you may meditate while engaged upon it. That eminent Christian saint and philosopher, Jacob Boehme, realized his vast knowledge of divine things whilst working long hours as a shoemaker. In every life there is time to think, and the busiest, the most laborious is not shut out from aspiration and meditation.

Spiritual meditation and self-discipline are inseparable; you will, therefore, commence to meditate upon yourself so as to try and understand yourself, for, remember, the great object you will have in view will be the complete removal of all your errors in order that you may realize Truth. You will begin to question your motives, thoughts, and acts, comparing them with your ideal, and endeavoring to look upon them with a calm and impartial eye. In this manner you will be continually gaining more of that mental and spiritual equilibrium without which men are but helpless straws upon the ocean of life. If you are given to hatred or anger you will meditate upon gentleness and forgiveness, so as to become acutely alive to a sense of your harsh and foolish conduct. You will then begin to dwell in thoughts of love, of gentleness, of abounding forgiveness; and as you overcome the lower by the higher, there will gradually, silently steal into your heart a knowledge of the divine Law of Love with an understanding of its bearing upon all the intricacies of life and conduct. And in applying this knowledge to your every thought, word, and act, you will grow more and more gentle, more and more loving, more and more divine. And thus with every error, every selfish desire, every human weakness; by the power of meditation is it overcome, and as each sin, each error is thrust out, a fuller and clearer measure of the Light of Truth illumines the pilgrim soul.

Thus meditating, you will be ceaselessly fortifying yourself against your only *real* enemy, your selfish, perishable self, and will be establishing yourself more and more firmly in the divine and imperishable self that is inseparable from Truth. The direct outcome of your meditations will be a calm, spiritual strength which will be your stay and resting-place in the struggle of life. Great is the overcoming power of holy thought, and the strength and knowledge gained in the hour of silent meditation will enrich the soul with saving remembrance in the hour of strife, of sorrow, or of temptation.

As, by the power of meditation, you grow in wisdom, you will relinquish, more and more, your selfish desires which are fickle, impermanent, and productive of sorrow and pain; and will take your stand, with increasing steadfastness and trust, upon unchangeable principles, and will realize heavenly rest.

The use of meditation is the acquirement of a knowledge of eternal principles, and the power which results from meditation is the ability to rest upon and trust those principles, and so become one with the Eternal. The end of meditation is, therefore, direct knowledge of Truth, God, and the realization of divine and profound peace.

Let your meditations take their rise from the ethical ground which you now occupy. Remember that you are to *grow* into Truth by steady perseverance. If you are an orthodox Christian, meditate ceaselessly upon the spotless purity and divine excellence of the character of Jesus, and apply his every precept to your inner life and outward conduct, so as to approximate more and more toward his perfection. Do not be as those religious ones, who, refusing to meditate upon the Law of Truth, and to put into practice the precepts given to them by their Master, are content to formally worship, to cling to their particular creeds, and to continue in the ceaseless round of sin and suffering. Strive to rise, by the power of meditation, above all selfish clinging to partial gods or party creeds; above dead formalities and lifeless ignorance. Thus walking the high way of wisdom, with mind fixed upon the spotless Truth, you shall know no halting-place short of the realization of Truth.

He who earnestly meditates first perceives a truth, as it were, afar off, and then realizes it by daily practice. It is only the doer of the Word of Truth that can know of the doctrine of Truth, for though by pure thought the Truth is perceived, it is only actualized by practice.

Said the divine Gautama, the Buddha, "He who gives himself up to vanity, and does not give himself up to meditation, forgetting the real aim of life and grasping at pleasure, will in time envy him who has exerted himself in meditation," and he instructed his disciples in the following "Five Great Meditations":—

"The first meditation is the meditation of love, in which you so adjust your heart that you long for the weal and welfare of all beings, including the happiness of your enemies.

"The second meditation is the meditation of pity, in which you think of all beings in distress, vividly representing in your imagination their sorrows and anxieties so as to arouse a deep compassion for them in your soul.

"The third meditation is the meditation of joy, in which you think of the prosperity of others, and rejoice with their rejoicings.

"The fourth meditation is the meditation of impurity, in which you consider the evil consequences of corruption, the effects of sin and diseases. How trivial often the pleasure of the moment, and how fatal its consequences.

"The fifth meditation is the meditation on serenity, in which you rise above love and hate, tyranny and oppression, wealth and want, and regard your own fate with impartial calmness and perfect tranquillity."

By engaging in these meditations the disciples of the Buddha arrived at a knowledge of the Truth. But whether you engage in these particular meditations or not matters little so long as your object is Truth, so long as you hunger and thirst for that righteousness which is a holy heart and a blameless life. In your meditations, therefore, let your heart grow and expand with ever-broadening love, until, freed from all hatred, and passion, and condemnation, it embraces the whole universe with thoughtful tenderness. As the flower opens its petals to receive the morning light, so open your soul more and more to the glorious light of Truth. Soar upward upon the wings of aspiration; be fearless, and believe in the loftiest possibilities. Believe that a life of absolute meekness is possible; believe that a life of stainless purity is possible; believe that a life of perfect holiness is possible; believe that the realization of the highest truth is possible. He who so believes, climbs rapidly the heavenly hills, whilst the unbelievers continue to grope darkly and painfully in the fog-bound valleys.

So believing, so aspiring, so meditating, divinely sweet and beautiful will be your spiritual experiences, and glorious the revelations that will enrapture your inward vision. As you realize the divine Love, the divine Justice, the divine Purity, the Perfect Law of Good, or God, great will be your bliss and deep your peace. Old things will pass away, and all things will become new. The veil of the material universe, so dense and impenetrable to the eye of error, so thin and gauzy to the eye of Truth, will be lifted and the spiritual universe will be revealed. Time will cease, and you will live only in Eternity. Change and

mortality will no more cause you anxiety and sorrow, for
you will become established in the unchangeable, and will
dwell in the very heart of immortality.

STAR OF WISDOM
Star that of the birth of Vishnu,
Birth of Krishna, Buddha, Jesus,
Told the wise ones, Heavenward looking,
Waiting, watching for thy gleaming
In the darkness of the night-time,
In the starless gloom of midnight;
Shining Herald of the coming
Of the kingdom of the righteous;
Teller of the Mystic story
Of the lowly birth of Godhead
In the stable of the passions,
In the manger of the mind-soul;
Silent singer of the secret
Of compassion deep and holy
To the heart with sorrow burdened,
To the soul with waiting weary:—
Star of all-surpassing brightness,
Thou again dost deck the midnight;
Thou again dost cheer the wise ones
Watching in the creedal darkness,
Weary of the endless battle
With the grinding blades of error;
Tired of lifeless, useless idols,
Of the dead forms of religions;
Spent with watching for thy shining;
Thou hast ended their despairing;
Thou hast lighted up their pathway;
Thou hast brought again the old Truths
To the hearts of all thy Watchers;
To the souls of them that love thee

Thou dost speak of Joy and Gladness,
Of the peace that comes of Sorrow.
Blessed are they that can see thee,
Weary wanderers in the Night-time;
Blessed they who feel the throbbing,
In their bosoms feel the pulsing
Of a deep Love stirred within them
By the great power of thy shining.
Let us learn thy lesson truly;
Learn it faithfully and humbly;
Learn it meekly, wisely, gladly,
Ancient Star of holy Vishnu,
Light of Krishna, Buddha, Jesus.

THE TWO MASTERS, SELF AND TRUTH

Upon the battlefield of the human soul two masters are ever contending for the crown of supremacy, for the kingship and dominion of the heart; the master of self, called also the "Prince of this world," and the master of Truth, called also the Father God. The master self is that rebellious one whose weapons are passion, pride, avarice, vanity, self-will, implements of darkness; the master Truth is that meek and lowly one whose weapons are gentleness, patience, purity, sacrifice, humility, love, instruments of Light.

In every soul the battle is waged, and as a soldier cannot engage at once in two opposing armies, so every heart is enlisted either in the ranks of self or of Truth. There is no half-and-half course; "There is self and there is Truth; where self is, Truth is not, where Truth is, self is not." Thus spake Buddha, the teacher of Truth, and Jesus, the manifested Christ, declared that "No man can serve two masters; for either he will hate the one and love the other; or else he will hold to the one, and despise the other. Ye cannot serve God and Mammon."

Truth is so simple, so absolutely undeviating and uncompromising that it admits of no complexity, no turning, no qualification. Self is ingenious, crooked, and, governed by subtle and snaky desire, admits of endless turnings and qualifications, and the deluded worshipers of self vainly imagine that they can gratify every worldly desire, and at the same time possess the Truth. But the lovers of Truth worship Truth with the sacrifice of self, and ceaselessly guard themselves against worldliness and self-seeking.

Do you seek to know and to realize Truth? Then you must be prepared to sacrifice, to renounce to the uttermost, for

Truth in all its glory can only be perceived and known when the last vestige of self has disappeared.

The eternal Christ declared that he who would be His disciple must "deny himself daily." Are you willing to deny yourself, to give up your lusts, your prejudices, your opinions? If so, you may enter the narrow way of Truth, and find that peace from which the world is shut out. The absolute denial, the utter extinction, of self is the perfect state of Truth, and all religions and philosophies are but so many aids to this supreme attainment.

Self is the denial of Truth. Truth is the denial of self. As you let self die, you will be reborn in Truth. As you cling to self, Truth will be hidden from you.

Whilst you cling to self, your path will be beset with difficulties, and repeated pains, sorrows, and disappointments will be your lot. There are no difficulties in Truth, and coming to Truth, you will be freed from all sorrow and disappointment.

Truth in itself is not hidden and dark. It is always revealed and is perfectly transparent. But the blind and wayward self cannot perceive it. The light of day is not hidden except to the blind, and the Light of Truth is not hidden except to those who are blinded by self.

Truth is the one Reality in the universe, the inward Harmony, the perfect Justice, the eternal Love. Nothing can be added to it, nor taken from it. It does not depend upon any man, but all men depend upon it. You cannot perceive the beauty of Truth while you are looking out through the eyes of self. If you are vain, you will color everything with your own vanities. If lustful, your heart and mind will be so clouded with the smoke and flames of passion, that everything will appear distorted through them. If proud and opinionative, you will see nothing in the whole universe except the magnitude and importance of your own opinions.

There is one quality which pre-eminently distinguishes the man of Truth from the man of self, and that is *humility*. To be not only free from vanity, stubbornness and egotism, but to regard one's own opinions as of no value, this indeed is true humility.

He who is immersed in self regards his own opinions as Truth, and the opinions of other men as error. But that humble Truth-lover who has learned to distinguish between opinion and Truth, regards all men with the eye of charity, and does not seek to defend his opinions against theirs, but sacrifices those opinions that he may love the more, that he may manifest the spirit of Truth, for Truth in its very nature is ineffable and can only be lived. He who has most of charity has most of Truth.

Men engage in heated controversies, and foolishly imagine they are defending the Truth, when in reality they are merely defending their own petty interests and perishable opinions. The follower of self takes up arms against others. The follower of Truth takes up arms against himself. Truth, being unchangeable and eternal, is independent of your opinion and of mine. We may enter into it, or we may stay outside; but both our defense and our attack are superfluous, and are hurled back upon ourselves.

Men, enslaved by self, passionate, proud, and condemnatory, believe their particular creed or religion to be the Truth, and all other religions to be error; and they proselytize with passionate ardor. There is but one religion, the religion of Truth. There is but one error, the error of self. Truth is not a formal belief; it is an unselfish, holy, and aspiring heart, and he who has Truth is at peace with all, and cherishes all with thoughts of love.

You may easily know whether you are a child of Truth or a worshiper of self, if you will silently examine your mind, heart, and conduct. Do you harbor thoughts of suspicion, enmity, envy, lust, pride, or do you strenuously fight against these? If the former, you are chained to self, no matter what religion you may profess; if the latter, you are a candidate for Truth, even though outwardly you may profess no religion. Are you passionate, self-willed, ever seeking to gain your own ends, self-indulgent, and self-centered; or are you gentle, mild, unselfish, quit of every form of self-indulgence, and are ever ready to give up your own? If the former, self is your master; if the latter, Truth is the object of your affection. Do you strive for riches? Do you fight, with passion, for your party? Do you lust for power and leadership? Are you given to ostentation and self-praise? Or have you given up the love of riches? Have you relinquished all strife? Are you content to take the lowest place, and to be passed by unnoticed? And have you ceased to talk about yourself and to regard yourself with self-complacent pride? If the former, even though you may imagine you worship God, the god of your heart is self. If the latter, even though you may withhold your lips from worship, you are dwelling with the Most High.

The signs by which the Truth-lover is known are unmistakable. Hear the Holy Krishna declare them, in Sir Edwin Arnold's beautiful rendering of the "Bhagavad Gita":—

"Fearlessness, singleness of soul, the will
Always to strive for wisdom; opened hand
And governed appetites; and piety,
And love of lonely study; humbleness,
Uprightness, heed to injure nought which lives
Truthfulness, slowness unto wrath, a mind
That lightly letteth go what others prize;
And equanimity, and charity
Which spieth no man's faults; and tenderness
Towards all that suffer; a contented heart,
Fluttered by no desires; a bearing mild,
Modest and grave, with manhood nobly mixed,

With patience, fortitude and purity;
An unrevengeful spirit, never given
To rate itself too high—such be the signs,
O Indian Prince! of him whose feet are set
On that fair path which leads to heavenly birth!"

When men, lost in the devious ways of error and self, have forgotten the "heavenly birth," the state of holiness and Truth, they set up artificial standards by which to judge one another, and make acceptance of, and adherence to, their own particular theology, the test of Truth; and so men are divided one against another, and there is ceaseless enmity and strife, and unending sorrow and suffering.

Reader, do you seek to realize the birth into Truth? There is only one way: *Let self die.* All those lusts, appetites, desires, opinions, limited conceptions and prejudices to which you have hitherto so tenaciously clung, let them fall from you. Let them no longer hold you in bondage, and Truth will be yours. Cease to look upon your own religion as superior to all others, and strive humbly to learn the supreme lesson of charity. No longer cling to the idea, so productive of strife and sorrow, that the Savior whom you worship is the only Savior, and that the Savior whom your brother worships with equal sincerity and ardor, is an impostor; but seek diligently the path of holiness, and then you will realize that every holy man is a savior of mankind.

The giving up of self is not merely the renunciation of outward things. It consists of the renunciation of the inward sin, the inward error. Not by giving up vain clothing; not by relinquishing riches; not by abstaining from certain foods; not by speaking smooth words; not by merely doing these things is the Truth found; but by giving up the spirit of vanity; by relinquishing the desire for riches; by abstaining from the lust of self-indulgence; by giving up all hatred, strife, condemnation, and self-seeking, and becoming gentle and pure at heart; by

doing these things is the Truth found. To do the former,
and not to do the latter, is pharisaism and hypocrisy,
whereas the latter includes the former. You may renounce
the outward world, and isolate yourself in a cave or in the
depths of a forest, but you will take all your selfishness
with you, and unless you renounce that, great indeed will
be your wretchedness and deep your delusion. You may
remain just where you are, performing all your duties, and
yet renounce the world, the inward enemy. To be in the
world and yet not of the world is the highest perfection, the
most blessed peace, is to achieve the greatest victory. The
renunciation of self is the way of Truth, therefore,

"Enter the Path; there is no grief like hate,
No pain like passion, no deceit like sense;
Enter the Path; far hath he gone whose foot
Treads down one fond offense."

As you succeed in overcoming self you will begin to see
things in their right relations. He who is swayed by any
passion, prejudice, like or dislike, adjusts everything to
that particular bias, and sees only his own delusions. He
who is absolutely free from all passion, prejudice,
preference, and partiality, sees himself as he is; sees others
as they are; sees all things in their proper proportions and
right relations. Having nothing to attack, nothing to
defend, nothing to conceal, and no interests to guard, he is
at peace. He has realized the profound simplicity of Truth,
for this unbiased, tranquil, blessed state of mind and heart
is the state of Truth. He who attains to it dwells with the
angels, and sits at the footstool of the Supreme. Knowing
the Great Law; knowing the origin of sorrow; knowing the
secret of suffering; knowing the way of emancipation in
Truth, how can such a one engage in strife or
condemnation; for though he knows that the blind,
self-seeking world, surrounded with the clouds of its own

illusions, and enveloped in the darkness of error and self, cannot perceive the steadfast Light of Truth, and is utterly incapable of comprehending the profound simplicity of the heart that has died, or is dying, to self, yet he also knows that when the suffering ages have piled up mountains of sorrow, the crushed and burdened soul of the world will fly to its final refuge, and that when the ages are completed, every prodigal will come back to the fold of Truth. And so he dwells in goodwill toward all, and regards all with that tender compassion which a father bestows upon his wayward children.

Men cannot understand Truth because they cling to self, because they believe in and love self, because they believe self to be the only reality, whereas it is the one delusion.

When you cease to believe in and love self you will desert it, and will fly to Truth, and will find the eternal Reality.

When men are intoxicated with the wines of luxury, and pleasure, and vanity, the thirst of life grows and deepens within them, and they delude themselves with dreams of fleshly immortality, but when they come to reap the harvest of their own sowing, and pain and sorrow supervene, then, crushed and humiliated, relinquishing self and all the intoxications of self, they come, with aching hearts to the one immortality, the immortality that destroys all delusions, the spiritual immortality in Truth.

Men pass from evil to good, from self to Truth, through the dark gate of sorrow, for sorrow and self are inseparable. Only in the peace and bliss of Truth is all sorrow vanquished. If you suffer disappointment because your cherished plans have been thwarted, or because someone has not come up to your anticipations, it is because you are clinging to self. If you suffer remorse for your conduct, it is because you have given way to self. If you are overwhelmed with chagrin and regret because of the attitude of someone else toward you, it is because you have been cherishing self. If you are wounded on account of what has been done to you or said of you, it is because you are walking in the painful way of self. All suffering is of self. All suffering ends in Truth. When you have entered into and realized Truth, you will no longer suffer disappointment, remorse, and regret, and sorrow will flee from you.

"Self is the only prison that can ever bind the soul;
Truth is the only angel that can bid the gates unroll;
And when he comes to call thee, arise and follow fast;
His way may lie through darkness, but it leads to light at last."

The woe of the world is of its own making. Sorrow purifies and deepens the soul, and the extremity of sorrow is the prelude to Truth.

Have you suffered much? Have you sorrowed deeply? Have you pondered seriously upon the problem of life? If so, you are prepared to wage war against self, and to become a disciple of Truth.

The intellectual who do not see the necessity for giving up self, frame endless theories about the universe, and call them Truth; but do thou pursue that direct line of conduct which is the practice of righteousness, and thou wilt realize the Truth which has no place in theory, and which never changes. Cultivate your heart. Water it continually with unselfish love and deep-felt pity, and strive to shut out from it all thoughts and feelings which are not in accordance with Love. Return good for evil, love for hatred, gentleness for ill-treatment, and remain silent when attacked. So shall you transmute all your selfish desires into the pure gold of Love, and self will disappear in Truth. So will you walk blamelessly among men, yoked with the easy yoke of lowliness, and clothed with the divine garment of humility.

O come, weary brother! thy struggling and striving
End thou in the heart of the Master of ruth;
Across self's drear desert why wilt thou be driving,
Athirst for the quickening waters of Truth

When here, by the path of thy searching and sinning,
Flows Life's gladsome stream, lies Love's oasis green?
Come, turn thou and rest; know the end and beginning,
The sought and the searcher, the seer and seen.

Thy Master sits not in the unapproached mountains,
Nor dwells in the mirage which floats on the air,
Nor shalt thou discover His magical fountains
In pathways of sand that encircle despair.
In selfhood's dark desert cease wearily seeking
The odorous tracks of the feet of thy King;
And if thou wouldst hear the sweet sound of His
speaking,
Be deaf to all voices that emptily sing.

Flee the vanishing places; renounce all thou hast;
Leave all that thou lovest, and, naked and bare,
Thyself at the shrine of the *Innermost* cast;
The Highest, the Holiest, the Changeless is there.

Within, in the heart of the Silence He dwelleth;
Leave sorrow and sin, leave thy wanderings sore;
Come bathe in His Joy, whilst He, whispering, telleth
Thy soul what it seeketh, and wander no more.

Then cease, weary brother, thy struggling and striving;
Find peace in the heart of the Master of ruth.
Across self's dark desert cease wearily driving;
Come; drink at the beautiful waters of Truth.

THE ACQUIREMENT OF SPIRITUAL POWER

The world is filled with men and women seeking pleasure, excitement, novelty; seeking ever to be moved to laughter or tears; not seeking strength, stability, and power; but courting weakness, and eagerly engaged in dispersing what power they have.

Men and women of real power and influence are few, because few are prepared to make the sacrifice necessary to the acquirement of power, and fewer still are ready to patiently build up character.

To be swayed by your fluctuating thoughts and impulses is to be weak and powerless; to rightly control and direct those forces is to be strong and powerful. Men of strong animal passions have much of the ferocity of the beast, but this is not power. The elements of power are there; but it is only when this ferocity is tamed and subdued by the higher intelligence that real power begins; and men can only grow in power by awakening themselves to higher and ever higher states of intelligence and consciousness.

The difference between a man of weakness and one of power lies not in the strength of the personal will (for the stubborn man is usually weak and foolish), but in that focus of consciousness which represents their states of knowledge.

The pleasure-seekers, the lovers of excitement, the hunters after novelty, and the victims of impulse and hysterical emotion lack that knowledge of principles which gives balance, stability, and influence.

A man commences to develop power when, checking his impulses and selfish inclinations, he falls back upon the higher and calmer consciousness within him, and begins to steady himself upon a principle. The realization of unchanging principles in consciousness is at once the source and secret of the highest power.

When, after much searching, and suffering, and sacrificing, the light of an eternal principle dawns upon the soul, a divine calm ensues and joy unspeakable gladdens the heart.

He who has realized such a principle ceases to wander, and remains poised and self-possessed. He ceases to be "passion's slave," and becomes a master-builder in the Temple of Destiny.

The man that is governed by self, and not by a principle, changes his front when his selfish comforts are threatened. Deeply intent upon defending and guarding his own interests, he regards all means as lawful that will subserve that end. He is continually scheming as to how he may protect himself against his enemies, being too self-centered to perceive that he is his own enemy. Such a man's work crumbles away, for it is divorced from Truth and power. All effort that is grounded upon self, perishes; only that work endures that is built upon an indestructible principle.

The man that stands upon a principle is the same calm, dauntless, self-possessed man under all circumstances. When the hour of trial comes, and he has to decide between his personal comforts and Truth, he gives up his comforts and remains firm. Even the prospect of torture and death cannot alter or deter him. The man of self regards the loss of his wealth, his comforts, or his life as the greatest calamities which can befall him. The man of principle looks upon these incidents as comparatively insignificant, and not to be weighed with loss of character, loss of Truth. To desert Truth is, to him, the only happening which can really be called a calamity.

It is the hour of crisis which decides who are the minions of darkness, and who the children of Light. It is the epoch of threatening disaster, ruin, and persecution which divides the sheep from the goats, and reveals to the reverential gaze of succeeding ages the men and women of power.

It is easy for a man, so long as he is left in the enjoyment of his possessions, to persuade himself that he believes in and adheres to the principles of Peace, Brotherhood, and Universal Love; but if, when his enjoyments are threatened, or he imagines they are threatened, he begins to clamor loudly for war, he shows that he believes in and stands upon, not Peace, Brotherhood, and Love, but strife, selfishness, and hatred.

He who does not desert his principles when threatened with the loss of every earthly thing, even to the loss of reputation and life, is the man of power; is the man whose every word and work endures; is the man whom the afterworld honors, reveres, and worships. Rather than desert that principle of Divine Love on which he rested, and in which all his trust was placed, Jesus endured the utmost extremity of agony and deprivation; and today the world prostrates itself at his pierced feet in rapt adoration.

There is no way to the acquirement of spiritual power except by that inward illumination and enlightenment which is the realization of spiritual principles; and those principles can only be realized by constant practice and application.

Take the principle of divine Love, and quietly and diligently meditate upon it with the object of arriving at a thorough understanding of it. Bring its searching light to bear upon all your habits, your actions, your speech and intercourse with others, your every secret thought and desire. As you persevere in this course, the divine Love will become more and more perfectly revealed to you, and your own shortcomings will stand out in more and more vivid contrast, spurring you on to renewed endeavor; and having once caught a glimpse of the incomparable majesty of that imperishable principle, you will never again rest in your weakness, your selfishness, your imperfection, but will pursue that Love until you have relinquished every discordant element, and have brought yourself into perfect harmony with it. And that state of inward harmony is spiritual power. Take also other spiritual principles, such as Purity and Compassion, and apply them in the same way, and, so exacting is Truth, you will be able to make no stay, no resting-place until the inmost garment of your soul is bereft of every stain, and your heart has become incapable of any hard, condemnatory, and pitiless impulse.

Only in so far as you understand, realize, and rely upon, these principles, will you acquire spiritual power, and that power will be manifested in and through you in the form of increasing dispassion, patience and equanimity.

Dispassion argues superior self-control; sublime patience is the very hall-mark of divine knowledge, and to retain an unbroken calm amid all the duties and distractions of life, marks off the man of power. "It is easy in the world to live after the world's opinion; it is easy in solitude to live after our own; but the great man is he who in the midst of the crowd keeps with perfect sweetness the independence of solitude."

Some mystics hold that perfection in dispassion is the source of that power by which miracles (so-called) are performed, and truly he who has gained such perfect control of all his interior forces that no shock, however great, can for one moment unbalance him, must be capable of guiding and directing those forces with a master-hand.

To grow in self-control, in patience, in equanimity, is to grow in strength and power; and you can only thus grow by focusing your consciousness upon a principle. As a child, after making many and vigorous attempts to walk unaided, at last succeeds, after numerous falls, in accomplishing this, so you must enter the way of power by first attempting to stand alone. Break away from the tyranny of custom, tradition, conventionality, and the opinions of others, until you succeed in walking lonely and erect among men. Rely upon your own judgment; be true to your own conscience; follow the Light that is within you; all outward lights are so many will-o'-the-wisps. There will be those who will tell you that you are foolish; that your judgment is faulty; that your conscience is all awry, and that the Light within you is darkness; but heed them not. If what they say is true the sooner you, as a searcher for wisdom, find it out the better, and you can only make the discovery by bringing your powers to the test. Therefore, pursue your course bravely. Your conscience is at least your own, and to follow it is to be a man; to follow the conscience of another is to be a slave. You will have many falls, will suffer many wounds, will endure many buffetings for a time, but press on in faith, believing that sure and certain victory lies ahead. Search for a rock, a principle, and having found it cling to it; get it under your feet and stand erect upon it, until at last, immovably fixed upon it, you succeed in defying the fury of the waves and storms of selfishness.

For selfishness in any and every form is dissipation, weakness, death; unselfishness in its spiritual aspect is conservation, power, life. As you grow in spiritual life, and become established upon principles, you will become as beautiful and as unchangeable as those principles, will taste of the sweetness of their immortal essence, and will realize the eternal and indestructible nature of the God within.

> No harmful shaft can reach the righteous man,
> Standing erect amid the storms of hate,
> Defying hurt and injury and ban,
> Surrounded by the trembling slaves of Fate.

> Majestic in the strength of silent power,
> Serene he stands, nor changes not nor turns;
> Patient and firm in suffering's darkest hour,
> Time bends to him, and death and doom he spurns.

Wrath's lurid lightnings round about him play,
And hell's deep thunders roll about his head;
Yet heeds he not, for him they cannot slay
Who stands whence earth and time and space are fled.

Sheltered by deathless love, what fear hath he?
Armored in changeless Truth, what can he know
Of loss and gain? Knowing eternity,
He moves not whilst the shadows come and go.

Call him immortal, call him Truth and Light
And splendor of prophetic majesty
Who bideth thus amid the powers of night,
Clothed with the glory of divinity.

THE REALIZATION OF SELFLESS LOVE

It is said that Michael Angelo saw in every rough block of stone a thing of beauty awaiting the master-hand to bring it into reality. Even so, within each there reposes the Divine Image awaiting the master-hand of Faith and the chisel of Patience to bring it into manifestation. And that Divine Image is revealed and realized as stainless, selfless Love.

Hidden deep in every human heart, though frequently covered up with a mass of hard and almost impenetrable accretions, is the spirit of Divine Love, whose holy and spotless essence is undying and eternal. It is the Truth in man; it is that which belongs to the Supreme: that which is real and immortal. All else changes and passes away; this alone is permanent and imperishable; and to realize this Love by ceaseless diligence in the practice of the highest righteousness, to live in it and to become fully conscious in it, is to enter into immortality here and now, is to become one with Truth, one with God, one with the central Heart of all things, and to know our own divine and eternal nature.

To reach this Love, to understand and experience it, one must work with great persistency and diligence upon his heart and mind, must ever renew his patience and keep strong his faith, for there will be much to remove, much to accomplish before the Divine Image is revealed in all its glorious beauty.

He who strives to reach and to accomplish the divine will be tried to the very uttermost; and this is absolutely necessary, for how else could one acquire that sublime patience without which there is no real wisdom, no divinity? Ever and anon, as he proceeds, all his work will seem to be futile, and his efforts appear to be thrown away. Now and then a hasty touch will mar his image, and perhaps when he imagines his work is almost completed he will find what he imagined to be the beautiful form of Divine Love utterly destroyed, and he must begin again with his past bitter experience to guide and help him. But he who has resolutely set himself to realize the Highest recognizes no such thing as defeat. All failures are apparent, not real. Every slip, every fall, every return to selfishness is a lesson learned, an experience gained, from which a golden grain of wisdom is extracted, helping the striver toward the accomplishment of his lofty object. To recognize

"That of our vices we can frame
A ladder if we will but tread
Beneath our feet each deed of shame,"

is to enter the way that leads unmistakably toward the Divine, and the failings of one who thus recognizes are so many dead selves, upon which he rises, as upon stepping-stones, to higher things.

Once come to regard your failings, your sorrows and sufferings as so many voices telling you plainly where you are weak and faulty, where you fall below the true and the divine, you will then begin to ceaselessly watch yourself, and every slip, every pang of pain will show you where you are to set to work, and what you have to remove out of your heart in order to bring it nearer to the likeness of the Divine, nearer to the Perfect Love. And as you proceed, day by day detaching yourself more and more from the inward selfishness the Love that is selfless will gradually become revealed to you. And when you are growing patient and calm, when your petulances, tempers, and irritabilities are passing away from you, and the more powerful lusts and prejudices cease to dominate and enslave you, then you will know that the divine is awakening within you, that you are drawing near to the eternal Heart, that you are not far from that selfless Love, the possession of which is peace and immortality.

Divine Love is distinguished from human loves in this supremely important particular, *it is free from partiality*. Human loves cling to a particular object to the exclusion of all else, and when that object is removed, great and deep is the resultant suffering to the one who loves. Divine Love embraces the whole universe, and, without clinging to any part, yet contains within itself the whole, and he who comes to it by gradually purifying and broadening his human loves until all the selfish and impure elements are burnt out of them, ceases from suffering. It is because human loves are narrow and confined and mingled with selfishness that they cause suffering. No suffering can result from that Love which is so absolutely pure that it seeks nothing for itself. Nevertheless, human loves are absolutely necessary as steps toward the Divine, and no soul is prepared to partake of Divine Love until it has become capable of the deepest and most intense human love. It is only by passing through human loves and human sufferings that Divine Love is reached and realized.

All human loves are perishable like the forms to which they cling; but there is a Love that is imperishable, and that does not cling to appearances.

All human loves are counterbalanced by human hates; but there is a Love that admits of no opposite or reaction; divine and free from all taint of self, that sheds its fragrance on all alike.

Human loves are reflections of the Divine Love, and draw the soul nearer to the reality, the Love that knows neither sorrow nor change.

It is well that the mother, clinging with passionate tenderness to the little helpless form of flesh that lies on her bosom, should be overwhelmed with the dark waters of sorrow when she sees it laid in the cold earth. It is well that her tears should flow and her heart ache, for only thus can she be reminded of the evanescent nature of the joys and objects of sense, and be drawn nearer to the eternal and imperishable Reality.

It is well that lover, brother, sister, husband, wife should suffer deep anguish, and be enveloped in gloom when the visible object of their affections is torn from them, so that they may learn to turn their affections toward the invisible Source of all, where alone abiding satisfaction is to be found.

It is well that the proud, the ambitious, the self-seeking, should suffer defeat, humiliation, and misfortune; that they should pass through the scorching fires of affliction; for only thus can the wayward soul be brought to reflect upon the enigma of life; only thus can the heart be softened and purified, and prepared to receive the Truth.

When the sting of anguish penetrates the heart of human love; when gloom and loneliness and desertion cloud the soul of friendship and trust, then it is that the heart turns toward the sheltering love of the Eternal, and finds rest in its silent peace. And whosoever comes to this Love is not turned away comfortless, is not pierced with anguish nor surrounded with gloom; and is never deserted in the dark hour of trial.

The glory of Divine Love can only be revealed in the heart that is chastened by sorrow, and the image of the heavenly state can only be perceived and realized when the lifeless, formless accretions of ignorance and self are hewn away.

Only that Love that seeks no personal gratification or reward, that does not make distinctions, and that leaves behind no heartaches, can be called divine.

Men, clinging to self and to the comfortless shadows of evil, are in the habit of thinking of divine Love as something belonging to a God who is out of reach; as something outside themselves, and that must for ever remain outside. Truly, the Love of God is ever beyond the reach of self, but when the heart and mind are emptied of self then the selfless Love, the supreme Love, the Love that is of God or Good becomes an inward and abiding reality.

And this inward realization of holy Love is none other than the Love of Christ that is so much talked about and so little comprehended. The Love that not only saves the soul from sin, but lifts it also above the power of temptation.

But how may one attain to this sublime realization? The answer which Truth has always given, and will ever give to this question is,—"Empty thyself, and I will fill thee." Divine Love cannot be known until self is dead, for self is the denial of Love, and how can that which is known be also denied? Not until the stone of self is rolled away from the sepulcher of the soul does the immortal Christ, the pure Spirit of Love, hitherto crucified, dead and buried, cast off the bands of ignorance, and come forth in all the majesty of His resurrection.

You believe that the Christ of Nazareth was put to death and rose again. I do not say you err in that belief; but if you refuse to believe that the gentle spirit of Love is crucified daily upon the dark cross of your selfish desires, then, I say, you err in this unbelief, and have not yet perceived, even afar off, the Love of Christ.

You say that you have tasted of salvation in the Love of Christ. Are you saved from your temper, your irritability, your vanity, your personal dislikes, your judgment and condemnation of others? If not, from what are you saved, and wherein have you realized the transforming Love of Christ?

He who has realized the Love that is divine has become a new man, and has ceased to be swayed and dominated by the old elements of self. He is known for his patience, his purity, his self-control, his deep charity of heart, and his unalterable sweetness.

Divine or selfless Love is not a mere sentiment or emotion; it is a state of knowledge which destroys the dominion of evil and the belief in evil, and lifts the soul into the joyful realization of the supreme Good. To the divinely wise, knowledge and Love are one and inseparable.

It is toward the complete realization of this divine Love that the whole world is moving; it was for this purpose that the universe came into existence, and every grasping at happiness, every reaching out of the soul toward objects, ideas and ideals, is an effort to realize it. But the world does not realize this Love at present because it is grasping at the fleeting shadow and ignoring, in its blindness, the substance. And so suffering and sorrow continue, and must continue until the world, taught by its self-inflicted pains, discovers the Love that is selfless, the wisdom that is calm and full of peace.

And this Love, this Wisdom, this Peace, this tranquil state of mind and heart may be attained to, may be realized by all who are willing and ready to yield up self, and who are prepared to humbly enter into a comprehension of all that the giving up of self involves. There is no arbitrary power in the universe, and the strongest chains of fate by which men are bound are self-forged. Men are chained to that which causes suffering because they desire to be so, because they love their chains, because they think their little dark prison of self is sweet and beautiful, and they are afraid that if they desert that prison they will lose all that is real and worth having.

"Ye suffer from yourselves, none else compels,   None other holds ye that ye live and die."

And the indwelling power which forged the chains and built around itself the dark and narrow prison, can break away when it desires and wills to do so, and the soul does will to do so when it has discovered the worthlessness of its prison, when long suffering has prepared it for the reception of the boundless Light and Love.

As the shadow follows the form, and as smoke comes after fire, so effect follows cause, and suffering and bliss follow the thoughts and deeds of men. There is no effect in the world around us but has its hidden or revealed cause, and that cause is in accordance with absolute justice. Men reap a harvest of suffering because in the near or distant past they have sown the seeds of evil; they reap a harvest of bliss also as a result of their own sowing of the seeds of good. Let a man meditate upon this, let him strive to understand it, and he will then begin to sow only seeds of good, and will burn up the tares and weeds which he has formerly grown in the garden of his heart.

The world does not understand the Love that is selfless because it is engrossed in the pursuit of its own pleasures, and cramped within the narrow limits of perishable interests mistaking, in its ignorance, those pleasures and interests for real and abiding things. Caught in the flames of fleshly lusts, and burning with anguish, it sees not the pure and peaceful beauty of Truth. Feeding upon the swinish husks of error and self-delusion, it is shut out from the mansion of all-seeing Love.

Not having this Love, not understanding it, men institute innumerable reforms which involve no inward sacrifice, and each imagines that his reform is going to right the world for ever, while he himself continues to propagate evil by engaging it in his own heart. That only can be called reform which tends to reform the human heart, for all evil has its rise there, and not until the world, ceasing from selfishness and party strife, has learned the lesson of divine Love, will it realize the Golden Age of universal blessedness.

Let the rich cease to despise the poor, and the poor to condemn the rich; let the greedy learn how to give, and the lustful how to grow pure; let the partisan cease from strife, and the uncharitable begin to forgive; let the envious endeavor to rejoice with others, and the slanderers grow ashamed of their conduct. Let men and women take this course, and, lo! the Golden Age is at hand. He, therefore, who purifies his own heart is the world's greatest benefactor.

Yet, though the world is, and will be for many ages to come, shut out from that Age of Gold, which is the realization of selfless Love, you, if you are willing, may enter it now, by rising above your selfish self; if you will pass from prejudice, hatred, and condemnation, to gentle and forgiving love.

Where hatred, dislike, and condemnation are, selfless Love does not abide. It resides only in the heart that has ceased from all condemnation.

You say, "How can I love the drunkard, the hypocrite, the sneak, the murderer? I am compelled to dislike and condemn such men." It is true you cannot love such men *emotionally*, but when you say that you must perforce dislike and condemn them you show that you are not acquainted with the Great over-ruling Love; for it is possible to attain to such a state of interior enlightenment as will enable you to perceive the train of causes by which these men have become as they are, to enter into their intense sufferings, and to know the certainty of their ultimate purification. Possessed of such knowledge it will be utterly impossible for you any longer to dislike or condemn them, and you will always think of them with perfect calmness and deep compassion.

If you love people and speak of them with praise until they in some way thwart you, or do something of which you disapprove, and then you dislike them and speak of them with dispraise, you are not governed by the Love which is of God. If, in your heart, you are continually arraigning and condemning others, selfless Love is hidden from you.

He who knows that Love is at the heart of all things, and has realized the all-sufficing power of that Love, has no room in his heart for condemnation.

Men, not knowing this Love, constitute themselves judge and executioner of their fellows, forgetting that there is the Eternal Judge and Executioner, and in so far as men deviate from them in their own views, their particular reforms and methods, they brand them as fanatical, unbalanced, lacking judgment, sincerity, and honesty; in so far as others approximate to their own standard do they look upon them as being everything that is admirable. Such are the men who are centered in self. But he whose heart is centered in the supreme Love does not so brand and classify men; does not seek to convert men to his own views, not to convince them of the superiority of his methods. Knowing the Law of Love, he lives it, and maintains the same calm attitude of mind and sweetness of heart toward all. The debased and the virtuous, the foolish and the wise, the learned and the unlearned, the selfish and the unselfish receive alike the benediction of his tranquil thought.

You can only attain to this supreme knowledge, this divine Love by unremitting endeavor in self-discipline, and by gaining victory after victory over yourself. Only the pure in heart see God, and when your heart is sufficiently purified you will enter into the New Birth, and the Love that does not die, nor change, nor end in pain and sorrow will be awakened within you, and you will be at peace.

He who strives for the attainment of divine Love is ever seeking to overcome the spirit of condemnation, for where there is pure spiritual knowledge, condemnation cannot exist, and only in the heart that has become incapable of condemnation is Love perfected and fully realized.

The Christian condemns the Atheist; the Atheist satirizes the Christian; the Catholic and Protestant are ceaselessly engaged in wordy warfare, and the spirit of strife and hatred rules where peace and love should be.

"He that hateth his brother is a murderer," a crucifier of the divine Spirit of Love; and until you can regard men of all religions and of no religion with the same impartial spirit, with all freedom from dislike, and with perfect equanimity, you have yet to strive for that Love which bestows upon its possessor freedom and salvation.

The realization of divine knowledge, selfless Love, utterly destroys the spirit of condemnation, disperses all evil, and lifts the consciousness to that height of pure vision where Love, Goodness, Justice are seen to be universal, supreme, all-conquering, indestructible.

Train your mind in strong, impartial, and gentle thought; train your heart in purity and compassion; train your tongue to silence and to true and stainless speech; so shall you enter the way of holiness and peace, and shall ultimately realize the immortal Love. So living, without seeking to convert, you will convince; without arguing, you will teach; not cherishing ambition, the wise will find you out; and without striving to gain men's opinions, you will subdue their hearts. For Love is all-conquering, all-powerful; and the thoughts, and deeds, and words of Love can never perish.

To know that Love is universal, supreme, all-sufficing; to be freed from the trammels of evil; to be quit of the inward unrest; to know that all men are striving to realize the Truth each in his own way; to be satisfied, sorrowless, serene; this is peace; this is gladness; this is immortality; this is Divinity; this is the realization of selfless Love.

I stood upon the shore, and saw the rocks
Resist the onslaught of the mighty sea,   And when I thought how all the countless shocks
They had withstood through an eternity,
I said, "To wear away this solid main

The ceaseless efforts of the waves are vain."

But when I thought how they the rocks had rent,
And saw the sand and shingles at my feet
(Poor passive remnants of resistance spent)
Tumbled and tossed where they the waters meet,
Then saw I ancient landmarks 'neath the waves,
And knew the waters held the stones their slaves.

I saw the mighty work the waters wrought
By patient softness and unceasing flow;
How they the proudest promontory brought
Unto their feet, and massy hills laid low;
How the soft drops the adamantine wall
Conquered at last, and brought it to its fall.

And then I knew that hard, resisting sin
Should yield at last to Love's soft ceaseless roll
Coming and going, ever flowing in
Upon the proud rocks of the human soul;
That all resistance should be spent and past,
And every heart yield unto it at last.

ENTERING INTO THE INFINITE

From the beginning of time, man, in spite of his bodily appetites and desires, in the midst of all his clinging to earthly and impermanent things, has ever been intuitively conscious of the limited, transient, and illusionary nature of his material existence, and in his sane and silent moments has tried to reach out into a comprehension of the Infinite, and has turned with tearful aspiration toward the restful Reality of the Eternal Heart.

While vainly imagining that the pleasures of earth are real and satisfying, pain and sorrow continually remind him of their unreal and unsatisfying nature. Ever striving to believe that complete satisfaction is to be found in material things, he is conscious of an inward and persistent revolt against this belief, which revolt is at once a refutation of his essential mortality, and an inherent and imperishable proof that only in the immortal, the eternal, the infinite can he find abiding satisfaction and unbroken peace.

And here is the common ground of faith; here the root and spring of all religion; here the soul of Brotherhood and the heart of Love,—that man is essentially and spiritually divine and eternal, and that, immersed in mortality and troubled with unrest, he is ever striving to enter into a consciousness of his real nature.

The spirit of man is inseparable from the Infinite, and can be satisfied with nothing short of the Infinite, and the burden of pain will continue to weigh upon man's heart, and the shadows of sorrow to darken his pathway until, ceasing from his wanderings in the dream-world of matter, he comes back to his home in the reality of the Eternal.

As the smallest drop of water detached from the ocean contains all the qualities of the ocean, so man, detached in consciousness from the Infinite, contains within him its likeness; and as the drop of water must, by the law of its nature, ultimately find its way back to the ocean and lose itself in its silent depths, so must man, by the unfailing law of his nature, at last return to his source, and lose himself in the great ocean of the Infinite.

To re-become one with the Infinite is the goal of man. To enter into perfect harmony with the Eternal Law is Wisdom, Love and Peace. But this divine state is, and must ever be, incomprehensible to the merely personal. Personality, separateness, selfishness are one and the same, and are the antithesis of wisdom and divinity. By the unqualified surrender of the personality, separateness and selfishness cease, and man enters into the possession of his divine heritage of immortality and infinity.

Such surrender of the personality is regarded by the worldly and selfish mind as the most grievous of all calamities, the most irreparable loss, yet it is the one supreme and incomparable blessing, the only real and lasting gain. The mind unenlightened upon the inner laws of being, and upon the nature and destiny of its own life, clings to transient appearances, things which have in them no enduring substantiality, and so clinging, perishes, for the time being, amid the shattered wreckage of its own illusions.

Men cling to and gratify the flesh as though it were going to last for ever, and though they try to forget the nearness and inevitability of its dissolution, the dread of death and of the loss of all that they cling to clouds their happiest hours, and the chilling shadow of their own selfishness follows them like a remorseless specter.

And with the accumulation of temporal comforts and luxuries, the divinity within men is drugged, and they sink deeper and deeper into materiality, into the perishable life of the senses, and where there is sufficient intellect, theories concerning the immortality of the flesh come to be regarded as infallible truths. When a man's soul is clouded with selfishness in any or every form, he loses the power of spiritual discrimination, and confuses the temporal with the eternal, the perishable with the permanent, mortality with immortality, and error with Truth. It is thus that the world has come to be filled with theories and speculations having no foundation in human experience. Every body of flesh contains within itself, from the hour of birth, the elements of its own destruction, and by the unalterable law of its own nature must it pass away.

The perishable in the universe can never become permanent; the permanent can never pass away; the mortal can never become immortal; the immortal can never die; the temporal cannot become eternal nor the eternal become temporal; appearance can never become reality, nor reality fade into appearance; error can never become Truth, nor can Truth become error. Man cannot immortalize the flesh, but, by overcoming the flesh, by relinquishing all its inclinations, he can enter the region of immortality. "God alone hath immortality," and only by realizing the God state of consciousness does man enter into immortality.

All nature in its myriad forms of life is changeable, impermanent, unenduring. Only the informing Principle of nature endures. Nature is many, and is marked by separation. The informing Principle is One, and is marked by unity. By overcoming the senses and the selfishness within, which is the overcoming of nature, man emerges from the chrysalis of the personal and illusory, and wings himself into the glorious light of the impersonal, the region of universal Truth, out of which all perishable forms come.

Let men, therefore, practice self-denial; let them conquer their animal inclinations; let them refuse to be enslaved by luxury and pleasure; let them practice virtue, and grow daily into high and ever higher virtue, until at last they grow into the Divine, and enter into both the practice and the comprehension of humility, meekness, forgiveness, compassion, and love, which practice and comprehension constitute Divinity.

"Good-will gives insight," and only he who has so conquered his personality that he has but one attitude of mind, that of good-will, toward all creatures, is possessed of divine insight, and is capable of distinguishing the true from the false. The supremely good man is, therefore, the wise man, the divine man, the enlightened seer, the knower of the Eternal. Where you find unbroken gentleness, enduring patience, sublime lowliness, graciousness of speech, self-control, self-forgetfulness, and deep and abounding sympathy, look there for the highest wisdom, seek the company of such a one, for he has realized the Divine, he lives with the Eternal, he has become one with the Infinite. Believe not him that is impatient, given to anger, boastful, who clings to pleasure and refuses to renounce his selfish gratifications, and who practices not good-will and far-reaching compassion, for such a one hath not wisdom, vain is all his knowledge, and his works and words will perish, for they are grounded on that which passes away.

Let a man abandon self, let him overcome the world, let him deny the personal; by this pathway only can he enter into the heart of the Infinite.

The world, the body, the personality are mirages upon the desert of time; transitory dreams in the dark night of spiritual slumber, and those who have crossed the desert, those who are spiritually awakened, have alone comprehended the Universal Reality where all appearances are dispersed and dreaming and delusion are destroyed.

There is one Great Law which exacts unconditional obedience, one unifying principle which is the basis of all diversity, one eternal Truth wherein all the problems of earth pass away like shadows. To realize this Law, this Unity, this Truth, is to enter into the Infinite, is to become one with the Eternal.

To center one's life in the Great Law of Love is to enter into rest, harmony, peace. To refrain from all participation in evil and discord; to cease from all resistance to evil, and from the omission of that which is good, and to fall back upon unswerving obedience to the holy calm within, is to enter into the inmost heart of things, is to attain to a living, conscious experience of that eternal and infinite principle which must ever remain a hidden mystery to the merely perceptive intellect. Until this principle is realized, the soul is not established in peace, and he who so realizes is truly wise; not wise with the wisdom of the learned, but with the simplicity of a blameless heart and of a divine manhood.

To enter into a realization of the Infinite and Eternal is to rise superior to time, and the world, and the body, which comprise the kingdom of darkness; and is to become established in immortality, Heaven, and the Spirit, which make up the Empire of Light.

Entering into the Infinite is not a mere theory or sentiment. It is a vital experience which is the result of assiduous practice in inward purification. When the body is no longer believed to be, even remotely, the real man; when all appetites and desires are thoroughly subdued and purified; when the emotions are rested and calm, and when the oscillation of the intellect ceases and perfect poise is secured, then, and not till then, does consciousness become one with the Infinite; not until then is childlike wisdom and profound peace secured.

Men grow weary and gray over the dark problems of life, and finally pass away and leave them unsolved because they cannot see their way out of the darkness of the personality, being too much engrossed in its limitations. Seeking to save his personal life, man forfeits the greater impersonal Life in Truth; clinging to the perishable, he is shut out from a knowledge of the Eternal.

By the surrender of self all difficulties are overcome, and there is no error in the universe but the fire of inward sacrifice will burn it up like chaff; no problem, however great, but will disappear like a shadow under the searching light of self-abnegation. Problems exist only in our own self-created illusions, and they vanish away when self is yielded up. Self and error are synonymous. Error is involved in the darkness of unfathomable complexity, but eternal simplicity is the glory of Truth.

Love of self shuts men out from Truth, and seeking their own personal happiness they lose the deeper, purer, and more abiding bliss. Says Carlyle—"There is in man a higher than love of happiness. He can do without happiness, and instead thereof find blessedness.

... Love not pleasure, love God. This is the Everlasting Yea, wherein all contradiction is solved; wherein whoso walks and works, it is well with him."

He who has yielded up that self, that personality that men most love, and to which they cling with such fierce tenacity, has left behind him all perplexity, and has entered into a simplicity so profoundly simple as to be looked upon by the world, involved as it is in a network of error, as foolishness. Yet such a one has realized the highest wisdom, and is at rest in the Infinite. He "accomplishes without striving," and all problems melt before him, for he has entered the region of reality, and deals, not with changing effects, but with the unchanging principles of things. He is enlightened with a wisdom which is as superior to ratiocination, as reason is to animality. Having yielded up his lusts, his errors, his opinions and prejudices, he has entered into possession of the knowledge of God, having slain the selfish desire for heaven, and along with it the ignorant fear of hell; having relinquished even the love of life itself, he has gained supreme bliss and Life Eternal, the Life which bridges life and death, and knows its own immortality. Having yielded up all without reservation, he has gained all, and rests in peace on the bosom of the Infinite.

Only he who has become so free from self as to be equally content to be annihilated as to live, or to live as to be annihilated, is fit to enter into the Infinite. Only he who, ceasing to trust his perishable self, has learned to trust in boundless measure the Great Law, the Supreme Good, is prepared to partake of undying bliss.

For such a one there is no more regret, nor disappointment, nor remorse, for where all selfishness has ceased these sufferings cannot be; and whatever happens to him he knows that it is for his own good, and he is content, being no longer the servant of self, but the servant of the Supreme. He is no longer affected by the changes of earth, and when he hears of wars and rumors of wars his peace is not disturbed, and where men grow angry and cynical and quarrelsome, he bestows compassion and love. Though appearances may contradict it, he knows that the world is progressing, and that

"Through its laughing and its weeping,
Through its living and its keeping,
Through its follies and its labors, weaving in and out of sight,
To the end from the beginning,
Through all virtue and all sinning,
Reeled from God's great spool of Progress, runs the golden
    thread of light."

When a fierce storm is raging none are angered about it, because they know it will quickly pass away, and when the storms of contention are devastating the world, the wise man, looking with the eye of Truth and pity, knows that it will pass away, and that out of the wreckage of broken hearts which it leaves behind the immortal Temple of Wisdom will be built.

Sublimely patient; infinitely compassionate; deep, silent, and pure, his very presence is a benediction; and when he speaks men ponder his words in their hearts, and by them rise to higher levels of attainment. Such is he who has entered into the Infinite, who by the power of utmost sacrifice has solved the sacred mystery of life.

Questioning Life and Destiny and Truth,
I sought the dark and labyrinthine Sphinx,
Who spake to me this strange and wondrous thing:—
"Concealment only lies in blinded eyes,
And God alone can see the Form of God."
 I sought to solve this hidden mystery
Vainly by paths of blindness and of pain,
But when I found the Way of Love and Peace,
Concealment ceased, and I was blind no more:
Then saw I God e'en with the eyes of God.

SAINTS, SAGES, AND SAVIORS: THE LAW OF SERVICE

The spirit of Love which is manifested as a perfect and rounded life, is the crown of being and the supreme end of knowledge upon this earth.

The measure of a man's truth is the measure of his love, and Truth is far removed from him whose life is not governed by Love. The intolerant and condemnatory, even though they profess the highest religion, have the smallest measure of Truth; while those who exercise patience, and who listen calmly and dispassionately to all sides, and both arrive themselves at, and incline others to, thoughtful and unbiased conclusions upon all problems and issues, have Truth in fullest measure. The final test of wisdom is this,—how does a man live? What spirit does he manifest? How does he act under trial and temptation? Many men boast of being in possession of Truth who are continually swayed by grief, disappointment, and passion, and who sink under the first little trial that comes along. Truth is nothing if not unchangeable, and in so far as a man takes his stand upon Truth does he become steadfast in virtue, does he rise superior to his passions and emotions and changeable personality.

Men formulate perishable dogmas, and call them Truth. Truth cannot be formulated; it is ineffable, and ever beyond the reach of intellect. It can only be experienced by practice; it can only be manifested as a stainless heart and a perfect life.

Who, then, in the midst of the ceaseless pandemonium of schools and creeds and parties, has the Truth? He who lives it. He who practices it. He who, having risen above that pandemonium by overcoming himself, no longer engages in it, but sits apart, quiet, subdued, calm, and self-possessed, freed from all strife, all bias, all condemnation, and bestows upon all the glad and unselfish love of the divinity within him.

He who is patient, calm, gentle, and forgiving under all circumstances, manifests the Truth. Truth will never be proved by wordy arguments and learned treatises, for if men do not perceive the Truth in infinite patience, undying forgiveness, and all-embracing compassion, no words can ever prove it to them.

It is an easy matter for the passionate to be calm and patient when they are alone, or are in the midst of calmness. It is equally easy for the uncharitable to be gentle and kind when they are dealt kindly with, but he who retains his patience and calmness under all trial, who remains sublimely meek and gentle under the most trying circumstances, he, and he alone, is possessed of the spotless Truth. And this is so because such lofty virtues belong to the Divine, and can only be manifested by one who has attained to the highest wisdom, who has relinquished his passionate and self-seeking nature, who has realized the supreme and unchangeable Law, and has brought himself into harmony with it.

Let men, therefore, cease from vain and passionate arguments about Truth, and let them think and say and do those things which make for harmony, peace, love, and good-will. Let them practice heart-virtue, and search humbly and diligently for the Truth which frees the soul from all error and sin, from all that blights the human heart, and that darkens, as with unending night, the pathway of the wandering souls of earth.

There is one great all-embracing Law which is the foundation and cause of the universe, the Law of Love. It has been called by many names in various countries and at various times, but behind all its names the same unalterable Law may be discovered by the eye of Truth. Names, religions, personalities pass away, but the Law of Love remains. To become possessed of a knowledge of this

Law, to enter into conscious harmony with it, is to become immortal, invincible, indestructible.

It is because of the effort of the soul to realize this Law that men come again and again to live, to suffer, and to die; and when realized, suffering ceases, personality is dispersed, and the fleshly life and death are destroyed, for consciousness becomes one with the Eternal.

The Law is absolutely impersonal, and its highest manifested expression is that of Service. When the purified heart has realized Truth it is then called upon to make the last, the greatest and holiest sacrifice, the sacrifice of the well-earned enjoyment of Truth. It is by virtue of this sacrifice that the divinely-emancipated soul comes to dwell among men, clothed with a body of flesh, content to dwell among the lowliest and least, and to be esteemed the servant of all mankind. That sublime humility which is manifested by the world's saviors is the seal of Godhead, and he who has annihilated the personality, and has become a living, visible manifestation of the impersonal, eternal, boundless Spirit of Love, is alone singled out as worthy to receive the unstinted worship of posterity. He only who succeeds in humbling himself with that divine humility which is not only the extinction of self, but is also the pouring out upon all the spirit of unselfish love, is exalted above measure, and given spiritual dominion in the hearts of mankind.

All the great spiritual teachers have denied themselves personal luxuries, comforts, and rewards, have abjured temporal power, and have lived and taught the limitless and impersonal Truth. Compare their lives and teachings, and you will find the same simplicity, the same self-sacrifice, the same humility, love, and peace both lived and preached by them. They taught the same eternal Principles, the realization of which destroys all evil. Those who have been hailed and worshiped as the saviors of mankind are manifestations of the Great impersonal Law,

and being such, were free from passion and prejudice, and
having no opinions, and no special letter of doctrine to
preach and defend, they never sought to convert and to
proselytize. Living in the highest Goodness, the supreme
Perfection, their sole object was to uplift mankind by
manifesting that Goodness in thought, word, and deed.
They stand between man the personal and God the
impersonal, and serve as exemplary types for the salvation
of self-enslaved mankind.

Men who are immersed in self, and who cannot
comprehend the Goodness that is absolutely impersonal,
deny divinity to all saviors except their own, and thus
introduce personal hatred and doctrinal controversy, and,
while defending their own particular views with passion,
look upon each other as being heathens or infidels, and so
render null and void, as far as their lives are concerned,
the unselfish beauty and holy grandeur of the lives and
teachings of their own Masters. Truth cannot be limited; it
can never be the special prerogative of any man, school, or
nation, and when personality steps in, Truth is lost.

The glory alike of the saint, the sage, and the savior is
this,—that he has realized the most profound lowliness,
the most sublime unselfishness; having given up all, even
his own personality, all his works are holy and enduring,
for they are freed from every taint of self. He gives, yet
never thinks of receiving; he works without regretting the
past or anticipating the future, and never looks for reward.

When the farmer has tilled and dressed his land and put
in the seed, he knows that he has done all that he can
possibly do, and that now he must trust to the elements,
and wait patiently for the course of time to bring about the
harvest, and that no amount of expectancy on his part will
affect the result. Even so, he who has realized Truth goes
forth as a sower of the seeds of goodness, purity, love and
peace, without expectancy, and never looking for results,
knowing that there is the Great Over-ruling Law which

brings about its own harvest in due time, and which is alike the source of preservation and destruction.

Men, not understanding the divine simplicity of a profoundly unselfish heart, look upon their particular savior as the manifestation of a special miracle, as being something entirely apart and distinct from the nature of things, and as being, in his ethical excellence, eternally unapproachable by the whole of mankind. This attitude of unbelief (for such it is) in the divine perfectibility of man, paralyzes effort, and binds the souls of men as with strong ropes to sin and suffering. Jesus "grew in wisdom" and was "perfected by suffering." What Jesus was, he became such; what Buddha was, he became such; and every holy man became such by unremitting perseverance in self-sacrifice. Once recognize this, once realize that by watchful effort and hopeful perseverance you can rise above your lower nature, and great and glorious will be the vistas of attainment that will open out before you. Buddha vowed that he would not relax his efforts until he arrived at the state of perfection, and he accomplished his purpose.

What the saints, sages, and saviors have accomplished, you likewise may accomplish if you will only tread the way which they trod and pointed out, the way of self-sacrifice, of self-denying service.

Truth is very simple. It says, "Give up self," "Come unto Me" (away from all that defiles) "and I will give you rest." All the mountains of commentary that have been piled upon it cannot hide it from the heart that is earnestly seeking for Righteousness. It does not require learning; it can be known in spite of learning. Disguised under many forms by erring self-seeking man, the beautiful simplicity and clear transparency of Truth remains unaltered and undimmed, and the unselfish heart enters into and partakes of its shining radiance. Not by weaving complex theories, not by building up speculative philosophies is Truth realized; but by weaving the web of inward purity, by building up the Temple of a stainless life is Truth realized.

He who enters upon this holy way begins by restraining his passions. This is virtue, and is the beginning of saintship, and saintship is the beginning of holiness. The entirely worldly man gratifies all his desires, and practices no more restraint than the law of the land in which he lives demands; the virtuous man restrains his passions; the saint attacks the enemy of Truth in its stronghold within his own heart, and restrains all selfish and impure thoughts; while the holy man is he who is free from passion and all impure thought, and to whom goodness and purity have become as natural as scent and color are to the flower. The holy man is divinely wise; he alone knows Truth in its fullness, and has entered into abiding rest and peace. For him evil has ceased; it has disappeared in the universal light of the All-Good. Holiness is the badge of wisdom. Said Krishna to the Prince Arjuna—

> "Humbleness, truthfulness, and harmlessness,
> Patience and honor, reverence for the wise,
> Purity, constancy, control of self,
> Contempt of sense-delights, self-sacrifice,
> Perception of the certitude of ill
> In birth, death, age, disease, suffering and sin;
> An ever tranquil heart in fortunes good
> And fortunes evil, ...
> ...Endeavors resolute
> To reach perception of the utmost soul,
> And grace to understand what gain it were
> So to attain—this is true wisdom, Prince!
> And what is otherwise is ignorance!"

Whoever fights ceaselessly against his own selfishness, and strives to supplant it with all-embracing love, is a saint, whether he live in a cottage or in the midst of riches and influence; or whether he preaches or remains obscure.

To the worldling, who is beginning to aspire towards higher things, the saint, such as a sweet St. Francis of Assisi, or a conquering St. Anthony, is a glorious and inspiring spectacle; to the saint, an equally enrapturing sight is that of the sage, sitting serene and holy, the conqueror of sin and sorrow, no more tormented by regret and remorse, and whom even temptation can never reach; and yet even the sage is drawn on by a still more glorious vision, that of the savior actively manifesting his knowledge in selfless works, and rendering his divinity more potent for good by sinking himself in the throbbing, sorrowing, aspiring heart of mankind.

And this only is true service—to forget oneself in love towards all, to lose oneself in working for the whole. O thou vain and foolish man, who thinkest that thy many works can save thee; who, chained to all error, talkest loudly of thyself, thy work, and thy many sacrifices, and magnifiest thine own importance; know this, that though thy fame fill the whole earth, all thy work shall come to dust, and thou thyself be reckoned lower than the least in the Kingdom of Truth!

Only the work that is impersonal can live; the works of self are both powerless and perishable. Where duties, howsoever humble, are done without self-interest, and with joyful sacrifice, there is true service and enduring work. Where deeds, however brilliant and apparently successful, are done from love of self, there is ignorance of the Law of Service, and the work perishes.

It is given to the world to learn one great and divine lesson, the lesson of absolute unselfishness. The saints, sages, and saviors of all time are they who have submitted themselves to this task, and have learned and lived it. All the Scriptures of the world are framed to teach this one lesson; all the great teachers reiterate it. It is too simple for the world which, scorning it, stumbles along in the complex ways of selfishness.

A pure heart is the end of all religion and the beginning of divinity. To search for this Righteousness is to walk the Way of Truth and Peace, and he who enters this Way will soon perceive that Immortality which is independent of birth and death, and will realize that in the Divine economy of the universe the humblest effort is not lost.

The divinity of a Krishna, a Gautama, or a Jesus is the crowning glory of self-abnegation, the end of the soul's pilgrimage in matter and mortality, and the world will not have finished its long journey until every soul has become as these, and has entered into the blissful realization of its own divinity.

Great glory crowns the heights of hope by arduous struggle won;
Bright honor rounds the hoary head that mighty works hath done;
Fair riches come to him who strives in ways of golden gain.
And fame enshrines his name who works with genius-glowing brain;
But greater glory waits for him who, in the bloodless strife
'Gainst self and wrong, adopts, in love, the sacrificial life;
And brighter honor rounds the brow of him who, 'mid the scorns
Of blind idolaters of self, accepts the crown of thorns;
And fairer purer riches come to him who greatly strives
To walk in ways of love and truth to sweeten human lives;
And he who serveth well mankind exchanges fleeting fame
For Light eternal, Joy and Peace, and robes of heavenly flame.

THE REALIZATION OF PERFECT PEACE

In the external universe there is ceaseless turmoil, change, and unrest; at the heart of all things there is undisturbed repose; in this deep silence dwelleth the Eternal.

Man partakes of this duality, and both the surface change and disquietude, and the deep-seated eternal abode of Peace, are contained within him.

As there are silent depths in the ocean which the fiercest storm cannot reach, so there are silent, holy depths in the heart of man which the storms of sin and sorrow can never disturb. To reach this silence and to live consciously in it is peace.

Discord is rife in the outward world, but unbroken harmony holds sway at the heart of the universe. The human soul, torn by discordant passion and grief, reaches blindly toward the harmony of the sinless state, and to reach this state and to live consciously in it is peace.

Hatred severs human lives, fosters persecution, and hurls nations into ruthless war, yet men, though they do not understand why, retain some measure of faith in the overshadowing of a Perfect Love; and to reach this Love and to live consciously in it is peace.

And this inward peace, this silence, this harmony, this Love, is the Kingdom of Heaven, which is so difficult to reach because few are willing to give up themselves and to become as little children.

"Heaven's gate is very narrow and minute,
It cannot be perceived by foolish men
Blinded by vain illusions of the world;
E'en the clear-sighted who discern the way,
And seek to enter, find the portal barred,
And hard to be unlocked. Its massive bolts

Are pride and passion, avarice and lust."

Men cry peace! peace! where there is no peace, but on the contrary, discord, disquietude and strife. Apart from that Wisdom which is inseparable from self-renunciation, there can be no real and abiding peace.

The peace which results from social comfort, passing gratification, or worldly victory is transitory in its nature, and is burnt up in the heat of fiery trial. Only the Peace of Heaven endures through all trial, and only the selfless heart can know the Peace of Heaven.

Holiness alone is undying peace. Self-control leads to it, and the ever-increasing Light of Wisdom guides the pilgrim on his way. It is partaken of in a measure as soon as the path of virtue is entered upon, but it is only realized in its fullness when self disappears in the consummation of a stainless life.

"This is peace,
To conquer love of self and lust of life,
To tear deep-rooted passion from the heart
To still the inward strife."

If, O reader! you would realize the Light that never fades, the Joy that never ends, and the tranquillity that cannot be disturbed; if you would leave behind for ever your sins, your sorrows, your anxieties and perplexities; if, I say, you would partake of this salvation, this supremely glorious Life, then conquer yourself. Bring every thought, every impulse, every desire into perfect obedience to the divine power resident within you. There is no other way to peace but this, and if you refuse to walk it, your much praying and your strict adherence to ritual will be fruitless and unavailing, and neither gods nor angels can help you. Only to him that overcometh is given the white stone of the regenerate life, on which is written the New and Ineffable Name.

Come away, for awhile, from external things, from the pleasures of the senses, from the arguments of the intellect, from the noise and the excitements of the world, and withdraw yourself into the inmost chamber of your heart, and there, free from the sacrilegious intrusion of all selfish desires, you will find a deep silence, a holy calm, a blissful repose, and if you will rest awhile in that holy place, and will meditate there, the faultless eye of Truth will open within you, and you will see things as they really are. This holy place within you is your real and eternal self; it is the divine within you; and only when you identify yourself with it can you be said to be "clothed and in your right mind." It is the abode of peace, the temple of wisdom, the dwelling-place of immortality. Apart from this inward resting-place, this Mount of Vision, there can be no true peace, no knowledge of the Divine, and if you can remain there for one minute, one hour, or one day, it is possible for you to remain there always. All your sins and sorrows, your fears and anxieties are your own, and you can cling to them or you can give them up. Of your own accord you cling to your unrest; of your own accord you can come to abiding peace. No one else can give up sin for you; you must give it up yourself. The greatest teacher can do no more than walk the way of Truth for himself, and point it out to you; you yourself must walk it for yourself. You can obtain freedom and peace alone by your own efforts, by yielding up that which binds the soul, and which is destructive of peace.

The angels of divine peace and joy are always at hand, and if you do not see them, and hear them, and dwell with them, it is because you shut yourself out from them, and prefer the company of the spirits of evil within you. You are what you will to be, what you wish to be, what you prefer to be. You can commence to purify yourself, and by so doing can arrive at peace, or you can refuse to purify yourself, and so remain with suffering.

Step aside, then; come out of the fret and the fever of life; away from the scorching heat of self, and enter the inward resting-place where the cooling airs of peace will calm, renew, and restore you.

Come out of the storms of sin and anguish. Why be troubled and tempest-tossed when the haven of Peace of God is yours!

Give up all self-seeking; give up self, and lo! the Peace of God is yours!

Subdue the animal within you; conquer every selfish uprising, every discordant voice; transmute the base metals of your selfish nature into the unalloyed gold of Love, and you shall realize the Life of Perfect Peace. Thus subduing, thus conquering, thus transmuting, you will, O reader! while living in the flesh, cross the dark waters of mortality, and will reach that Shore upon which the storms of sorrow never beat, and where sin and suffering and dark uncertainty cannot come. Standing upon that Shore, holy, compassionate, awakened, and self-possessed and glad with unending gladness, you will realize that

"Never the Spirit was born, the Spirit will cease to be never;

Never was time it was not, end and beginning are dreams;

Birthless and deathless and changeless remaineth the Spirit for ever;

Death hath not touched it at all, dead though the house of it seems."

You will then know the meaning of Sin, of Sorrow, of Suffering, and that the end thereof is Wisdom; will know the cause and the issue of existence.

And with this realization you will enter into rest, for this
is the bliss of immortality, this the unchangeable gladness,
this the untrammeled knowledge, undefiled Wisdom, and
undying Love; this, and this only, is the realization of
Perfect Peace.

O thou who wouldst teach men of Truth!
Hast thou passed through the desert of doubt?
Art thou purged by the fires of sorrow? hath ruth
The fiends of opinion cast out
Of thy human heart? Is thy soul so fair
That no false thought can ever harbor there?
O thou who wouldst teach men of Love!
Hast thou passed through the place of despair?
Hast thou wept through the dark night of grief?
does it move
(Now freed from its sorrow and care)
Thy human heart to pitying gentleness,
Looking on wrong, and hate, and ceaseless stress?
O thou who wouldst teach men of Peace!
Hast thou crossed the wide ocean of strife?
Hast thou found on the Shores of the Silence,
Release from all the wild unrest of life?
From thy human heart hath all striving gone,
Leaving but Truth, and Love, and Peace alone?